marketplace christianity

DISCOVERING THE KINGDOM PURPOSES OF THE MARKETPLACE

BY ROBERT FRASER

Marketplace Christianity: Discovering the Kingdom Purposes of the Marketplace (2nd Edition)

International Standard Book Number: 978-0-9753905-1-1

Published by:

New Grid Publishing
11184 Antioch #354
Overland Park, KS 66210

For additional copies, visit www.newgridbooks.com.

Second Printing.

Edited by Joel Kilpatrick

dedication

This book is dedicated to Lauren,
my wife and best friend of twenty years.
Thank you for faithfully and lovingly walking with me
through this earthly journey.
You have made sweet,
what otherwise would have been unbearable.

acknowledgements

I would like to thank Joel Kilpatrick for his help in writing this book.

Also, thank you, Bob Hartley for helping me refine and articulate this message and for being a "redeemer of lost purpose" in my life.

Thank you, Mike Bickle for blazing a trail of intimacy with God and inviting everyone to the party (as well as the fast!), and for throwing open the doors of opportunity.

Thank you, Mike Frank for encouraging me in this message.

Thank you, Lisa Sangster for your tireless joy and energy in getting this book and a thousand other things off the ground.

Thank you, Bob Sorge for your invaluable wisdom and counsel to me as a writer.

free study guide

For a free Marketplace Christianity study guide, register online at:
www.josephcompany.org/mc/

contents

marketplace christianity

foreword

The vast majority of the Church is comprised of marketplace people. They lead full, busy lives with 40 plus hours of work per week. Because their lives are necessarily less engaged in church activities, they have been traditionally viewed as less spiritual, causing them often to feel as if they are second-class spiritual citizens in the Kingdom of God.

This disenfranchisement of marketplace people has had many tragic effects upon the body of Christ. They find themselves spiritually bored and unsure of their gifts and callings. They lack a biblical understanding of how to blend passionate spirituality with their vocation. Most importantly, they have lost their sense of spiritual purpose and significance. This lack of vision has kept our marketplace people from taking their places of spiritual leadership, and as a result the church remains unprepared for the crises that face us in the decades ahead.

God is breathing on those like Bob Fraser who have a tried and tested vision for deep spirituality and passion for Jesus in the marketplace. He brings a fresh new understanding through his anointed business model that is based solidly on biblical foundations, as well as experiential knowledge. Bob masterfully bridges the gap between the board room and the prayer room with simple, profound principles that bring eternal meaning back into the daily experience of each employee, from the clerk in the mailroom to the most high-powered executive. Bob experienced a five-year revival within the business he began and grew to over 250 employees. As his pastor during this period, I personally saw hundreds of lives deeply impacted by this extraordinary company. He brilliantly describes how easily vibrant, full Christian community erupts from the marketplace when the principles of the anointed business model are employed.

Bob has a profound grasp of the critical role that Christians in the marketplace will play in the end time scenario that is rapidly unfolding. As well as addressing the subjects of creating wealth, the transfer of wealth into the Kingdom of God, and building cities of refuge, he also delves deeply into the heart attitudes and disciplines so necessary to succeed in the end time shaking, such as holiness, purity of motive, and the fasted lifestyle.

This new understanding of the value and potential of the marketplace is exploding as God draws attention to it through such anointed vessels as Bob Fraser. The implications for the cause of evangelism alone in the anointed business model are staggering. We have seen this model in action here at the International House of Prayer in Kansas City where Bob directs The Joseph Company. I have seen his students become successful entrepreneurs through the Goshen Business Incubator and heard powerful testimonies of lives impacted. I highly commend this book to you as a powerful tool for gaining understanding and recapturing vision for the possibilities of your spiritual destiny in the marketplace.

Mike Bickle,

Director, International House of Prayer of Kansas City

CHAPTER ONE

crisis in the marketplace

I was studying computer science at one of the best engineering schools in the world, the University of California at Berkeley. I was in the top of my class and had one quarter of study left before I graduated, which is like saying I had the football and an empty field before me. The future was open and full of rewards just waiting to be claimed. But I was about to derail my own career. Less than a year earlier I'd experienced something that threw me into a life-altering crisis from which I would never recover.

I'd given my heart to God one Easter Sunday at the small Catholic parish next to my fraternity house. It was a bold move for a boy who'd grown up a "devout" atheist, who'd mocked Christians at school for being too weak to handle the "truth" of a godless universe. My family never set foot in church, and I never had a single thought toward God as a child.

But after my conversion I redefined my life in the most radical way, and God became my sole focus. I was baptized and filled with the Holy Spirit and drank from the scriptures as one might drink from a fire hose, taking in every word and then starting all over again. I stopped filling my notebooks with diagrams and instead filled thousands of pages with notes on the Bible. My passion for God grew into a raging fire.

Consumed by a desire to serve God, I told my pastor I was quitting Berkeley. "God doesn't care about computers," I told him. "They're not part of the Kingdom." He encouraged me to finish since I only had one quarter left, and I acquiesced, but in my mind the purpose of my life had completely changed. Once, I'd dreamed of following my ambitions into the workplace, perhaps starting a business or becoming an entrepreneur, but now I narrowed my goals to one: I was going to become a senior pastor. That, I believed, was what you did if you were wholehearted for God.

Two years later I attained that dream and became the senior pastor of a small campus church. With great confidence that I was God's gift to ministry, I evangelized, preached, sang, even wrote the songs. I loved it…I was in my own private heaven, and apparently I was there alone. After less than a year, I was fired. I was stunned.

I was told my deficiency was training, so I moved myself and my family to Los Angeles where I studied for the ministry. To pay the bills, I got a non-ministry job, but I felt like a spiritual failure. I went to work, but only for the money. I had no vision for myself in the workplace. It seemed a spiritual wasteland. My wife and I spent all our available time leading home groups and Bible studies, evangelizing, teaching, pastoring and discipling many. And yet my calling for God remained frustrated. It would be years before I realized God had given me a passion, but He had not called me to vocational ministry, He had called me to the marketplace. I was not a pastor – I was a *Marketplace Christian.*

Frustrated Passion

For people who are passionate for Jesus, there are dozens of well-trod paths into ministry but few into the marketplace. Have you ever heard someone say, "I'm so passionate for Jesus, I just have to go into business"? Why don't we hear that? Because, without ever saying so, most Christians believe that a marketplace vocation and passion for Jesus are mutually exclusive. This is one of the great tragedies of modern Christianity, and it has robbed millions of people of their passion and purpose, and robbed the Son of God of His inheritance in us. And yet, before the books close on history we will see an army of believers who do say, "I am so passionate for Jesus I must go into the marketplace." We will see passion fully expressed in the realm of business and entrepreneurship in such a way that we'll wonder how the Church survived without it.

> For people who are passionate for Jesus, there are dozens of well-trod paths into ministry but few into the marketplace

Early in my career, I didn't comprehend that I could fulfill my passion for Jesus through being an engineer. I had never seen it modeled. I had no idea that a Christian could take his or her passion into the marketplace and let it flourish in ways that would affect the world as much as any sermon or song. I was told by a leader that he thought I would be a "pastor of a business." I was insulted by what I perceived as a second-class calling – I wanted to be a "real pastor." To me, full-time ministry was the only way to serve God to the fullest and highest measure.

I'm convinced that thousands of Christians feel the same frustration. Countless numbers throw themselves into vocational ministry, exhausting themselves in a type of work they were not designed or gifted for because they believe passion for Jesus demands it. They are wholehearted, but misguided. They are in danger of missing their marketplace calling.

Countless numbers throw themselves into vocational ministry, exhausting themselves in a type of work they were not designed or gifted for because they believe passion for Jesus demands it

Those who do end up in the marketplace often feel like spiritual failures, as if they have somehow compromised their faith, or chosen a lesser path. Years later, when I started my business, a back-office e-commerce provider for thousands of business customers including Xerox, Chase Manhattan Bank and Samsung, I hired scores of such "failures," many of them Bible school graduates who had "hit a wall" in their pursuit of vocational ministry. They came to me, heads hung in shame, fully convinced they were ministry rejects. Of course, God had not rejected them; they just hadn't realized they were marketplace Christians, not vocational ministers.

The Only Calling?

It may surprise many to learn that nowhere in scripture are Christians told to go into vocational ministry. The only scripture that touches this topic approaches it very softly:

[1]If anyone sets his heart on being an overseer, he desires a noble task. 1 Tim. 3:1 (NIV)

In fact, the Bible explicitly teaches the *opposite*:

[21]Were you called while a slave? Do not worry about it; but if you are able also to become free, rather do that. [24]Brethren, each one is to remain with God in that condition in which he was called. 1 Cor. 7:21,24 (NASB)

> **There is no vocation we can choose that we cannot fully experience God and fulfill a holy calling**

We are instructed to "remain *with God* in that condition" in which we were called. *God has no desire to take believers out of their arena of life* and into a spiritual bunker where their faith is safe. Neither does He want us simply to endure our vocation while experiencing Him only in church meetings. We are to remain in our vocation, *with God*. It is His strategy that we would stay where we are and invite God into our situation.

There is no vocation in which we cannot *fully* experience God and fulfill a holy calling. Conversely, there is no vocation, including vocational ministry, that *guarantees* we will experience God and fulfill a holy calling. God is not confined to our parameters. He is not only the God of church but also the God of all of life. Our goal and purpose is to find where we fit and pursue him passionately and wholeheartedly from that place.

A Crisis of Vision

Most Marketplace Christians feel spiritually purposeless, meaningless, and aimless. They often fail to appreciate their value or understand practically how to bring the Kingdom of God into their vocation. Only about three percent of Christians are called to vocational ministry, and yet the current church teachings have not helped the other 97 percent develop a vision for what they do. Instead, they have been told their only purpose is giving financially. In essence, their role is *engaging in the worthless in order to give financially to the worthy.*

Marketplace Christians are often encouraged to stop spending so much time in marketplace activities and throw themselves into ministry activities. The message is that marketplace activities are devoid of spiritual purpose. Christians can best express their love for Jesus, they are told, by coming to church meetings, volunteering with the youth, teaching Sunday school, ushering, greeting and so on. For the typical Marketplace Christian, these activities amount to perhaps 1 percent of their lives. What about the other 99 percent? It's subtly implied that this doesn't "count" as ministry.

> **In essence, their role is engaging in the worthless in order to give financially to the worthy**

It is no different for stay-at-home parents. Marketplace Christians are not just those who have paying jobs, but those who participate in any arena of life outside of church. My wife, Lauren, is a passionate, uncompromising believer, actively ministering and evangelizing whenever she can. But as our family grew, she found herself increasingly tied to the home and buried by the responsibilities of children. For years she struggled with the same sense of meaninglessness and worthlessness, because she was not able to minister but just occasionally. The church's message — that life outside of narrowly-defined ministry activities is throwaway, meaningless, or merely mundane — affected her just as it affects Christian businessmen and entrepreneurs.

A People with No Heroes

I am an avid reader of biographies. On my wall is an entire shelf of biographies about great Christians. But one day I gazed at the rows of books and realized that almost all our modern Christian heroes are vocational ministers: Rees Howells, David Brainerd, George Muller, Charles Wesley, Finney, Jonathan Edwards, John Calvin, Smith Wigglesworth, Mother Theresa — the list goes on.

In contrast, most biblical heroes *were not priests*. Abraham was a rancher and a businessman; Joseph was a businessman and a skilled administrator. Joshua and Caleb were generals; David was a shepherd, a general, and a king; Daniel and Nehemiah were governmental administrators. But these biblical heroes have been

biblical heroes have been interpreted for us through the eyes of modern-day priests and they have been stripped of their marketplace identity

interpreted for us through the eyes of modern-day priests and they have been stripped of their marketplace identity.

Modern Christianity lacks models of passion for Jesus in the marketplace. Models turn abstract ideas into concrete, understandable realities. They demonstrate what can be done, how it's done, and in so doing they blow a hole through present understanding so that millions of other people can follow into fresh territory. But think: If you wanted to be passionate in the marketplace, who would you be like? Who would you emulate? Who are the role models for Marketplace Christians? There are very few, and without models we can't envision what we are to do, much less walk it out.

Modern Christianity lacks models of passion for Jesus in the marketplace

In the marketplace, we have been robbed of our Kingdom heroes. The enemy has stolen those visions of greatness. Where are the mighty men and women of the marketplace who do exploits for God in the context of the workplace and home? Tragically, without such heroes, we have abdicated spiritual greatness to the priests. We must not give up our passion for the pursuit of spiritual greatness. God is again raising up modern-day Abrahams, Daniels, Nehemiahs and Josephs – normal, everyday people, who function in the marketplace, and who will mark history with their love for Jesus.

A Crisis of Value

Marketplace Christians lack more than vision and heroes; they often lack value within the church. One Christian man had booked $100 million dollars in international consulting contracts for his firm. He could have been a terrific marketplace hero, but instead he related that he sat in the back pew of a 50-member congregation and felt like a second-class citizen. There are hundreds, even thousands like him. They feel like the black sheep of God's family. Even if they succeed in the marketplace, it's conveyed to them in hundreds of subtle ways that their love for Jesus isn't good enough. The only value they seem to have is in what they give. My hope is that Marketplace Christians press in to become the most generous of givers; but the idea that a person's value is the size of his or her pocketbook means that rich Christians are more valuable than poor ones, which is both unbiblical and offensive.

This crisis of value affects both sides of the equation. While most Marketplace Christians feel like spiritual failures at some level, they also feel they are being obedient to their calling. They see themselves as courageous pioneers, but few understand *why* their gifts are valuable to the kingdom of God and *how* they fit His plan. There is a pitiful dearth of teaching on this subject. In fact, most ministers *do* value Marketplace Christians, but they have not developed the language or understanding to articulate the value of the marketplace, and so they unwittingly neutralize those called to carry the Gospel there.

> **They see themselves as courageous pioneers, but few understand *why* their gifts are valuable to the kingdom of God and *how* they fit His plan**

Businesspeople are *sought after* and *flattered*, but rarely *loved* and *supported*. A friend of mine had a dream about Marketplace Christians. They seemed to him like people who "so wanted to love God, but didn't know how to love Him." In the dream, a group of Marketplace Christians was drowning in the ocean, waves crashing over them. On the beach a group of ministers looked on. One turned to another and joked, "We should take their pocketbooks so they would float better."

This speaks of the relative insensitivity of many ministers to the struggles of Marketplace Christians. This insensitivity is not due to lack of love, but lack of understanding. The marketplace is perceived as troubled and volatile – businesses rise and fall, and that's "just business." A few years ago a generous Marketplace Christian gave $750,000 to a ministry I work with. We were overjoyed to receive it, and it enabled us to construct a ministry center. Two years later we touched base with this man and he apologized for not giving more gifts, but immediately after giving his previous contribution, he was severely persecuted and his business was suddenly taken out. It occurred to me how little we pray for Marketplace Christians. If this man had gone in for toe surgery, prayer chains would have been activated, but when facing a crushing attack on his business, he was left alone.

> **If this man had gone in for toe surgery, prayer chains would have been activated, but when facing a crushing attack on his business, he was left alone**

When my business encountered tough times, I felt the same way. Bad things were happening, many of us were under enormous stress, and I faced critical decisions whose consequences could have threatened the company. The business had hired hundreds of

Christians and given thousands of dollars to church work, but I felt I had nowhere to turn for real support. There was always a listening ear, but no call to action, no circling of the wagons, no banding together as brothers or sisters in battle. If my venture failed, apparently that was just part of doing business.

Why does any of this matter? This crisis in the marketplace has at least three tragic consequences:

Result #1: The Church's Inheritance is Stolen

As we'll see in later chapters, the marketplace is God's breeding ground of leadership, His repository of resources, and much more. If we continue to allow our marketplace breadwinners to fall at the enemy's hands, we will be breadless in our hour of need and will lack anointed leadership when the world desperately needs it from the church.

We must understand that the church's inheritance is to be the church of all of life, not just the bunker. Bunker Christianity — where people keep most ministry activity within the walls of the sanctuary, striving for better meetings and programs — is costing the church its inheritance. We're to inhabit the planet, not self-segregate and hunker down.

Result #2: God's Inheritance is Stolen

It's a great tragedy that marketplace saints have been robbed of their inheritance. But a worse tragedy is that it's not our inheritance that is stolen, but "His inheritance in us" (Eph 1:18).

When we fail to fulfill our calling, Jesus fails to receive the worship He is due. When Marketplace Christians don't connect to their purpose, they wander aimlessly, beaten down, distracted by pleasure, never lifting their voices in a stunning heart of love and worship.

God also loses the opportunity to perform awesome and massive mercy deeds and miracles through them. Someday, hundreds of thousands of Marketplace Christians will do astonishing feats of compassion, building mercy and food centers in other nations and more even beyond our present dreams. It's not happening now because we have no vision for it. The enemy has taken us out of contention.

> **When marketplace Christians don't connect to their purpose, they wander aimlessly, beaten down**

Finally, God's purpose in filling the earth with His glory is frustrated. He says, "As surely as I live," declares the Lord, "the *whole earth* will be filled with the glory of the Lord." (Num. 14:21) He is not going to let this idea go! The entire planet will be subdued and filled with the glory of God. The church has missed it when we say He can only be God of the bunker — the God of Sunday school, homeless shelters and Passion plays. His inheritance is much bigger than we've allowed it to be. He will be the God of the marketplace, the cities, the corner shop and the movie theaters, the schools, military bases, Fortune 500 companies, public parks, grocery stores, video rental stores and every other sphere. His glory will fill the earth!

Result #3: We Act Like the Disinherited

Many ministers have discouraged their leaders from going into the marketplace because they have seen passion wane and hearts grow cold in those who have chosen marketplace vocations. They see the marketplace as a "black hole" of faith.

Those fears are oftentimes justified. When Marketplace Christians disconnect from the church, whether out of impatience or because of the church's lack of love and support, they find their love grows cold, their faith dies, and they pursue money as an end in itself and idle pleasure as a right. They become independent.

> They act the part of the disinherited because they don't realize their own value

Many marketplace saints have not managed the garden of their hearts well. Without a vision they wander aimlessly and perish (Prov. 29:18), pursuing money and idleness because they have no other purpose. Why not pursue pleasure when everything else seems meaningless? Purpose always focuses on "self" unless there is a greater purpose to live for. But many Marketplace Christians don't know how to walk out their passion in everyday life, so the passion wilts. Their love dies because it finds no expression. Their hearts get stopped up, their faith shrinks. In short, they act the part of the disinherited because they don't realize their own value and nobody tells them they're valuable. Like a beautiful girl who is repeatedly told she's ugly and worthless until she believes those lies, so Marketplace Christians have believed a lie about their critical role in the life of the Kingdom.

But we live in days like Nehemiah's. Back then, the temple had been built – true worship had been restored – but there was no city, no commerce, education, government or community. In other words, there was no marketplace. As a result, the enemy ran roughshod over the people. History tells us Jerusalem was mostly abandoned (Neh. 7:4). The Jews scratched out a living in outlying areas, coming into the city to worship, but existing mostly isolated from one another, subject to the whims and cruelty of the local warlords. Without the city there was no strength of community, no corporate will, no resources, no ability to build permanent and sustainable lives.

The presence of God *will* be established in the marketplace and in the entire earth

But Nehemiah rebuilt the walls of the city and resettled it (Neh. 11:1). In our day, God wants to rebuild the *temple* of God, and the *city* of God as well. The temple is the church arena; the city is the marketplace, the homes, education, government, arts, culture and military. The church must reverse its abandonment of the marketplace. We have handed it over to the enemy without much of a fight. We have lost faith that God can inhabit the marketplace. We have built spiritual bunkers and practiced safe Christianity, relying on good attendance, good meetings and good programs as our barometer of success.

But God is the God of all areas of life, not just the church. The presence of God *will* be established in the marketplace and in the entire earth, but we must do our part to destroy false paradigms the church holds about the marketplace. We must get Marketplace Christians to lift up their eyes and see the vision God has for them in marketplace ministry. We must equip ministers with language, understanding and vision so they will stop unwittingly undermining Marketplace Christians. And we must establish models of passion in the marketplace. As we do, we will usher in the presence of God to the marketplace, redeeming it for Jesus, for the church and for the world.

So just how *does* the marketplace fit in God's Kingdom? In the next chapter we will see its critical importance as we will explore a few of the ways God uses the marketplace.

ten kingdom things business can do

I n 1995 I started NetSales, Inc., out of spiritual boredom, because ministry doors had closed to me. I had no vision for marketplace ministry. Over the next several years, NetSales grew and was blessed. I raised $44 million in investment capital and guided the company to an average 20 percent month-to-month revenue growth over six years, becoming the Kansas City metro area's fastest growing company between 1997 and 1999. In 2000, I was awarded the Midwest Region Ernst & Young Entrepreneur of the Year award.

But instead of feeling good about this success, I felt more and more chagrined. It was becoming clear that this was my lot in life – I was never going to be in ministry. My dream was dying. *I was relegated to spiritual insignificance.* I journeyed through this painful time, praying all the while, and I began to realize that God's opinion of significance might be different from mine. If my job was meaningful to Him, then my heart could be satisfied, regardless of what others thought, and even apart from what I thought. I finally was able to pray sincerely, "Lord, if you show me that this business is significant to you, then I will embrace it with my whole heart."

To my astonishment, the company soon became a center of Kingdom life and activity. A revival took place. It was not dramatic, but it was undeniable, and it went on for five years. I was nothing short of astonished. The business, of course, was a normal, everyday business, doing some things right and plenty of things wrong. We dealt with the same problems of disgruntled employees, quality deficiencies, mistakes and perturbed customers as any business does. It was laughable to think that anything "qualified" us for some special move of God, and indeed many in the company were neither aware of nor touched by the heightened spiritual activity. But the activity of the Kingdom of God was nevertheless taking place before my very eyes. I had hired a number of believers who were in a similar spiritual place as me. Though called to the marketplace, they were not aware of their calling. They had tried vocational ministry, coming to me only after they'd "failed" at it. But in our workplace they discovered a different kind of anointing and began walking in the presence and joy of God. They stumbled into a new place of ministry and saw dozens of people get saved. They grew in God,

They grew in God, grew in life skills, grew in maturity and gifting. They ministered daily, and discovered they were fulfilling the greatest commandments — in the marketplace

grew in life skills, grew in maturity and gifting. They ministered daily and discovered they were fulfilling the greatest commandments — in the marketplace.

I began to see that business is ordained of God to actually establish certain dimensions of the Kingdom of God. There are certain Kingdom things *only the marketplace can do*, certain fruit only business can produce which cannot be produced in ministries and ministry programs. I call these the Ten Kingdom Things Business Can Do, and they arise directly from my practical, workaday experience running a business with 280 employees.

> **Business is ordained of God to actually establish certain dimensions of the Kingdom of God**

1. Life Skills

There's a certain set of abilities people need to succeed in any arena of life. I call them life skills, and they include the ability to work well with people, maintain a good work ethic, solve problems, be diligent, persevere, follow through, resolve conflict, communicate, manage people, manage projects, have confidence, be teachable, motivate others, recruit, plan, make decisions and exercise good judgment. Often, the very best leaders are not the smartest or most talented people, but those with the strongest life skills. And even very talented and anointed individuals find their success firmly capped when they have poor life skills.

How are life skills acquired and developed? Most of us learned basic life skills from our parents at home. Sometimes we developed them further at church. But the greatest development of life skills typically comes from the marketplace.

Good businesses are life-skills factories. They make their trade in identifying, training, modeling and rewarding life skills. My life is a good example of this. Early in my career, I had exceptionally poor life skills. I was fired from several jobs, and I often created a negative "wake" behind me. But my business career reshaped me into an effective leader with passable life skills. It then became one of my great joys as CEO to watch passionate but "raw" Christians develop valuable life skills and soar to new personal heights.

Good businesses are life-skills factories

Strong life-skills are required for success in any vocation, including ministry. I believe many vocational ministers fail to achieve their spiritual potential because of underdeveloped life skills. One of my friends is full of passion and big dreams, but he has been a secondary-level ministry leader for twenty years. While he is an excellent communicator and has a heart of gold, he has poorly developed life skills, and this weakness has cost him many opportunities. If ten years ago he had taken a few years and worked a marketplace job for a good company, I have little doubt his ministry today would be vastly more effective, instead of being frustrated by low ceilings and closed doors. In him I see where I would be if I had not been fired from my pastoral position twenty years ago.

2. Leadership Development

There are many leaders in the church world, but the great preponderance of gifted leaders is in the marketplace. In business, true leaders are almost always welcomed as "rainmakers," those who will bring success in the future. Good leadership is rightly understood as the goose that lays the golden eggs. Most businesses have fast tracks for potential leaders, where they are mentored and given choice opportunities under watchful eyes. The best businesses master the ability to identify and develop leaders.

Leaders, by definition, think strategically, not just tactically. They anticipate and solve problems in advance instead of reacting to crises as they arise. Conversely, organizations without strong leadership tend to operate tactically, solving problems as they come up. For example, a ministry might scramble to find finances to build a new facility, but spend little or no effort training and releasing the wealth-creators of tomorrow.

In business, strategic thinking is not just good, it's a necessity. Without it, no business can last. Strategic thinking is often "out-of-the-box" and requires the organization to change with a changing environment. I have worked with hundreds of successful enterprises, and every one had a stable of strategic thinkers. The best strategic thinkers God has created are in the marketplace. This subject of leadership is so important to the church's success that we'll talk about it more in a later chapter.

3. Management Skill

While leaders create energy and activity, managers harness activity and bring productivity. Where there is leadership without management, there is *activity without productivity*. A leader provides the *vision*; a manager provides the *plan*. Without good management there is chaos, inefficiency, poor results and frustrated people.

> **Where there is leadership without management, there is activity without productivity**

When I evaluate the management effectiveness of a company, I ask these four questions:

Are the managers creating order by designing systems and processes?

Are there clearly defined roles and goals within the company?

Are workers empowered within certain boundaries?

What is the workplace's level of confusion and inefficiency?

Good management is absolutely critical in achieving any goal, if more than a few people are involved. Yet in many organizations, including many churches and ministries, good management is woefully absent. Anyone familiar with the "behind-the-scenes" operation of more than a few organizations has probably witnessed astonishing waste and mismanagement. I personally have watched ministry leaders (and plenty of businesses, too) throw more people and money at failing projects, all for naught. Without good management, all the resources in the world will be wasted.

I have rarely seen a good business embark on a major undertaking without a solid plan, carefully reviewed and refined by the key leaders. But weakly managed organizations rarely embark on a major undertaking *with* a plan. These leaders often assume that intensity of activity will result in productivity, and they are content with any results they get, even pitiful results.

Good managers form the backbone of good business, and so good businesses necessarily become management developing machines

Good managers form the backbone of good business, and so good businesses necessarily become management developing machines. Good managers know the importance of planning, and they can spot a good plan from a bad one. Their skills are invaluable to the church because without them, all the resources God sends will be frittered away.

4. Mentoring and Discipleship

Mentoring and discipleship are core missions for believers *and* for business. The best businesses recognize the importance of mentoring and devote significant internal resources to it. They usually call it "management training."

But church-based discipleship programs, while helpful, are inherently limited. They are limited in their ability to improve a person's life-skills because there is not enough real-life contact to encourage lasting change. Similarly, they can't effectively address character issues like self-centeredness, dishonesty, irresponsibility, a political spirit, anger and laziness because these issues rarely surface in a church setting.

But in business, these negative issues surface as a matter of course. Identifying them and developing remediation plans and accountability is standard management practice. Businesses, then, play a unique supplementary role in people's spiritual health and character development.

One friend of mine runs a large construction company. He is has a strong pastoral gifting – he could be a successful senior pastor in any church in the country. But instead of pastoring a church, he pastors his business. He is passionate about mentoring and discipling people. When he hires a new employee, he tells them about their "discipleship" practices: "We believe in addressing any issues in our employees that are limiting their potential." Then he asks them, "Are you personally willing to have this kind of input into your life?" Because they want the job, of course they respond enthusiastically! Then when issues of character or performance arise, he is able to address them directly and personally. In his 40+ years running his business, he has seen hundreds of lives transformed. At one time he thought he should go into vocational ministry to do "God's work." But today he says he has far more

At one time he thought he should go into vocational ministry to do "God's work." But today he says he has far more ministry opportunities and ministry reach than any pastor he knows.

ministry opportunities and ministry reach than any pastor he knows.

Mentoring and discipleship do more than address negative issues. They create opportunities, internships and apprenticeships, and they model success. This is stock-in-trade for businesses but is virtually impossible for a church to do except in the ministry arena.

Ultimately, mentoring and discipleship are about helping members of the next generation find their individual callings. Mentoring and discipleship are the tonic for purposelessness, one of the most spiritually debilitating and painful conditions a person can experience. As spiritual fathers and mothers, there are few joys greater than helping young people identify their heart desires, then helping them find their direction. This is one of the strengths of business, and it was one of my great joys as a CEO. Often I would hire a young, directionless person into an entry-level position. Once they were working, I could evaluate their giftings and callings and ultimately find a position that suited them perfectly. Even if I could not offer them a better position, I could give them a very clear sense of who they were and what I perceived God had placed in them. When I did have a position to offer them appropriate to their heart desires and giftings, I had the extreme pleasure of watching them discover their calling and begin to soar.

Business can also be a great vehicle to reach out and minister to troubled areas that need renewal and transformation. One day when I was reviewing businesses for sale I ran across an inner-city gas station and convenience store. They were asking $350,000, but it earned $250,000 per year in profit. I immediately thought of friends I know who love to minister to people in the inner city.

They give out food and clothing, which helps temporarily, but are unable to bring lasting change into people's lives. But if they owned a business like this, they could hire troubled teens, addicts, or people just needing a job to get on their feet, and use the job as means to truly disciple people. As bosses, we have a great ability to create opportunities for people and to speak constructively and authoritatively into their lives – so much more than someone giving them a meal. And as a side benefit, they could earn $250,000 per year! That's the power of mentoring and discipleship in the marketplace.

> **As bosses, we have a great ability to create opportunities for people and to speak constructively and authoritatively into their lives**

5. Everyman, Everyday Ministry

A few years ago during a church service I looked over several thousand faces sitting impassively in their chairs listening to the sermon. Many of them were powerful, anointed people in their own right, yet they seemed spiritually constipated. A question struck me: How much spiritual potential was being achieved in that room at that moment? Maybe one percent, I thought, and that was a generous estimate. If I was anywhere close to being right, it pointed to a terrific tragedy within the church.

Modern church has become meeting-oriented and ministry program-oriented, mostly because leaders want their churches to be considered dynamic and relevant. But by emphasizing meetings and programs, they have unwittingly undermined and disempowered the individual ministry taking place in homes and workplaces. In contrast, authentic, historic, biblical Christianity was not practiced primarily in church meetings but at home and in the marketplace. Meetings and ministry programs were so little thought of that believers had to be warned not to drop them altogether (Heb 10:25).

The traditional church model has been ineffective in unlocking everyday Christians' spiritual potential. Meetings can create knowledge, but do nothing to get believers to actually exercise their "faith muscle."

> **Authentic, historic, biblical Christianity was not practiced primarily in church meetings but at home and in the marketplace**

I believe the New Testament church was framed by apostolic power and preaching, but was built on everyman, everyday ministry, meaning all believers, even the youngest and least anointed, simply loved God and served others every day, in everything they did. I saw this kind of ministry take place at my business as our mini-revival unfolded. In fact, I was amazed to see the amount of ministry going forth. And it wasn't just one or two especially bold or gifted people – it was the majority of the believers. Many who could not find a place of effective ministry in the church setting found it in the workplace. Most of the believers had a job to do, and did it "as for the Lord" (Ephesians 6:7). But at the same time, most became friends with their "cube-mates;" they shared the gospel, shared their lives, prayed for each other and stood by each other during times of financial and family strain. The believers invited people to church, helped some get into church counseling programs, visited co-workers at the hospital and shared meals together. It's impossible to measure the "level" of ministry that was taking place, but one thing was clear: normal, everyday believers were walking in their spiritual potential to a high degree.

For a while I ran a business internship for young adults. In order to teach the interns about work, we opened a coffee cart in a local movie theater. I taught them two things. First, when they made a cup of coffee, they were to make it "with their *whole* heart, as for the *Lord*" (Eph. 6:7) – that is, as much as possible, with love flowing from their hearts back to Jesus. By doing this, I taught them they could fulfill the greatest commandment, "to love the Lord with all your heart" (Matt 22:36-40).

This is called *work*: fulfilling the two greatest commandments and getting paid twice.

Second, I taught them that when they served a customer they were to love them as fully and completely as possible, and in so doing, they would fulfill the second greatest commandment, "to love your neighbor as yourself" (Matt. 22:36-40).

In exchange for fulfilling the two greatest commandments, not only would God reward them (Eph. 6:8), but I would pay them too. This is called *work*: fulfilling the two greatest commandments and getting paid twice.

If the millions of marketplace believers who are operating at one percent of their spiritual potential were empowered to walk in even fifty percent of their spiritual potential, there would be a massive release of spiritual power in the earth. Everyday, everyman ministry would again be the driving force in church life.

6. Evangelism

As a young man, I preached open-air, handed out tracts, set up booths on campus, held on-campus Bible studies, performed servant evangelism, participated in debates and concerts, hosted meals for international students and knocked on doors. I yelled, I whispered, I wept, I prayed loudly, and I prayed silently. But none of it was as effective as what took place years later in my business.

Within five years, dozens of people were saved and the Lord touched hundreds who drew closer to knowing Him. As real friendships developed between employees and with customers, the gospel surfaced as a topic of legitimate conversation. Unlike non-relational evangelism, such as my open-air preaching and handing out tracts, this interaction was natural, comfortable and easy. Many believers, not just the bold ones, freely shared their lives and testimonies. I discovered that evangelism is totally different in the context of friendship. When a non-believer works alongside a believer and observes him or her truly "working as for the Lord" as it says in Colossians 3:23, their hearts open up. Trust develops. Personal testimonies, though rough and unpolished, carry weight when people know and respect the Christian people who speak them. Authentic faith in the context of genuine relationship never fails to deeply impact hearts.

Authentic faith in the context of genuine relationship never fails to deeply impact hearts

A friend of mine runs a community bank in Minnesota which has become one of the fastest growing banks in the country. But more amazingly, in the first 18 months the bank was opened, 102 people prayed to receive Christ – *in a bank*. When a secular magazine sent a writer to do a story on the bank, the writer gave his life to Jesus. When they sent a photographer, he too gave his life to Christ. More recently a delegation of bankers came from a communist country to study American banking. In my friend's office, they all prayed to receive Christ.

The workplace is a great harvest field. Billy Graham has said, "I believe one of the next great moves of God is going to be through the believers in the workplace." I agree. As believers embrace the simple biblical mandate of "working as for the Lord," we will witness a tremendous revival. God has laid the blueprints for this revival in the scriptures, but up to now these truths have been all but lost. The church has feared and abdicated the marketplace, lost its vision for marketplace evangelism, and therefore lost the very revival it seeks.

Marketplace evangelism will cross national borders to reach the world

Marketplace evangelism will cross national borders to reach the world. Increasingly, doors are closed to traditional missionaries – I believe by God's design. At the same time, doors are being thrown open to international businesses. I received a letter from a businessman who owns a food processing company. He was invited to start a branch of his business in China, where it would employ 6,000 displaced workers. In this scenario, he could start the business, bring a senior team of believers and build an "anointed business" which provides for 6,000 people, ministers to them and blesses the nation. Furthermore, they could share the gospel with relative impunity because they are a business. At this point in China, massive revival is underway only in rural areas. Perhaps marketplace ministry is God's strategy to bring the gospel into urban China and other hard-to-reach places on the globe.

7. Spiritual Oasis

When Christians gather together and "work as for the Lord" as the Bible mandates, it creates a spiritual oasis of Kingdom life. Christians feel free to spontaneously pray for one another. Bible studies erupt. Life-transforming teachings are modeled and are passed from person to person.

> When Christians gather together and "work as for the Lord" as the Bible mandates, it creates a spiritual oasis of Kingdom life

In our business, Christians were strengthened – the weak grew stronger, the strong, stronger still. Backsliders were returned to the fold. Passion for Jesus, modeled so well in a few, spread through the ranks. People supported and stood with one another through health woes, financial distress, family heartaches, drug and alcohol addictions and all kinds of emotional brokenness. Lives were touched and transformed, not by professional pastors, but by everyday Christians.

The presence of God was often manifested. One visitor who had been waiting in the lobby asked me what was different about the company. "People just seem so…happy," he stammered. "There is such a wonderful atmosphere here." He had been deeply touched by the presence of God and couldn't quantify it. Without realizing it, he'd stepped into a spiritual oasis in the middle of the marketplace.

Others are intentionally creating hotbeds of spiritual activity for the needy.

One lady long had a desire to minister to the mentally ill. She started her own mental care facility and hired Christian workers who shared her passion. Hundreds of people have been ministered to, people with this heart of compassion have wonderful jobs, and it is all funded by government programs.

Another group started a private prison, to handle overflow from regional government prisons, at significant cost savings to the government agencies. But more than that, it has become a ministry center where outreach programs run continually, helping thousands at perhaps their greatest points of personal crisis. Many have turned to Christ for the first time. Other nominal believers, once in prison, are confronted with the foolishness of their sin and return wholeheartedly to Christ, becoming fervent and fully abandoned in their faith – because they have nothing left to lose. To observe their prayer meetings is overwhelming, intense and powerful.

Many find a place of sanctuary. One prostitute who has been a regular "customer," confided one day, "this prison is the only place where I feel peace and where I feel safe."

These places have become spiritual oases, outposts of vibrant life and health, providing respite, refreshing, and sanctuary – in the middle of the marketplace.

8. Benevolence

One of the greatest opportunities in business is to help people in need. I recall a fellow church member and father of five coming to me one day, having hit rock-bottom. He said, "If you can pay me ten dollars per hour, I'll do anything you need, including scrubbing toilets." I hired him, and he was able to get back on his feet. A year later he left to work for another company for a nearly-six-figure salary.

One of my friends, a realtor, started a program called "Safe Harbor" to place single parent families in safe affordable homes with no money down. So far he has placed six families. Lenders and builders have rallied behind the program. Amazingly, it requires no donors – the program is completely self-sustaining. As such it can grow without limits, unlike donor-based programs.

One CEO says this about benevolence whenever someone asks him what he "does:" "I support widows and orphans, and help build the Kingdom of God," he says. "How I do that currently is through developing and selling software."

Another friend runs a large mortgage banking firm, specializing in helping people get out of debt and building equity in their homes. But her greatest passion is giving to those who care for abandoned children and who spread the gospel. She has structured her business so that it is 90% owned by a non-profit foundation – so

90% of her profits automatically go to missions. At the end of every month, she writes a check for whatever is left in the bank. She bases her life on the scripture:

[33]Sell your possessions and give to the poor. Provide purses for yourselves that will not wear out, a treasure in heaven that will not be exhausted, where no thief comes near and no moth destroys. Luke 12:33 (NIV)

She gives almost everything away and trusts God to take care of her. She calls it "banking with God." She says, "Why would you put your money in a bank where it is at-risk? When you 'bank with God' – giving it all to God – you know it is safe, because he will always take care of you." Not surprisingly, her revenues have tripled every year.

Caring for the poor is a critical biblical concept. In the scriptures, business was to care for the poor through the concept of gleaning – business owners were to leave behind some of the harvest for the poor who provided for themselves by harvesting the leftovers. The brilliance of gleaning is that it is not charity. It lets the poor help themselves, and can be the beginning of getting a life back on track. Several friends of mine make a point of leaving low-level jobs open for anyone who might be in need – a modern version of gleaning.

9. Friendship and Community

When people left our company, I would often ask what was the number one thing they appreciated about it. The top response by far was the friends they had made and the sense of community they felt.

Humans are designed to be in community together, but in modern society, true community can be hard to come by. Neighborhoods are not as community-oriented as they once were. Neighbors might live a few doors apart and never see each others' faces.

The workplace is a natural community

Church can be a difficult place to develop community because people spend so little time together. But the workplace is a natural community. People spend forty hours a week together in the "foxhole," working side by side, forming teams and setting and achieving goals. As a result, they bond together as an organic, functioning community.

10. Individual Wealth Creation and Kingdom Financing

Though I have emphasized the non-financial fruits of business, business is also meant to provide money for families and Kingdom projects. In my business, thirty or so families bought their first family house while employed with us. I hired many Christians who had been earning $15-30,000 per year in dead-end, low-paying jobs. Not only did they discover a calling, an anointing and a place of spiritual life and ministry, but they also prospered financially.

We hired one special young lady into our phone center for $10 per hour. She grew in anointing and skill, and within a couple years was hired away by another company for a six-figure salary.

Through the marketplace God is not only releasing individual wealth to meet the everyday needs of families, but he is also releasing enormous wealth – power to affect regions and nations:

[18] "But you shall remember the LORD your God, for it is He who is giving you power to make wealth, that He may confirm His covenant which He swore to your fathers. Deuteronomy 8:18 (NASB)

In order to fulfill his promise to Abraham, God must give to us the power to make wealth.

According to scripture, it is *God* who gives to individuals the power to create wealth, to *confirm his covenant.* He is referring to the promise he made to Abraham, to "make him a great nation" (Gen. 12:2). As Abraham's spiritual offspring, it is through *us* he must fulfill his promises to Abraham. Thus, in order to fulfill his promise to Abraham, God must give to us the power to make wealth.

God will release this wealth through supernatural ability and creativity. As Mike Bickle says, "you are one idea away from a billion dollars." The bible calls this kind of ability and creativity "wisdom." For example, when God gave Bezalel supernatural ability and creativity to build the tabernacle, he called it "wisdom" (Ex 31:3). And scripture boldly declares God is the source of all wisdom:

³in [Christ] are hidden all the treasures of wisdom and knowledge.
Colossians 2:3 (NIV)

All creative ideas come from God and he gives them to whomever he pleases. God will give supernatural ability to create wealth to those who have stopped building their own kingdom and who will use this power to establish *his* Kingdom on earth.

One friend had a great passion to give extravagantly to missions work. But his business partner strongly opposed this vision. My friend was shocked and perplexed when the business hit financial troubles and he found himself ousted. Why would God take away his only means of giving, his greatest passion? Wondering what to do next, he began to seek God in prayer with a renewed vigor and determination. Not long into this "wilderness" season, he and a friend discovered an amazing new technology that dramatically increases oil recovery from oil fields. It is easily a billion-dollar discovery. They believe that they have received the "power to make wealth" directly from God; and in the fear of God they are but stewards of his great gift.

> **God will give supernatural ability to create wealth to those who have stopped building their own kingdom and who will use this power to establish *his* Kingdom on earth.**

These ten Kingdom things a business can do can truly only be reproduced in the marketplace. God has structured life so that business should play a central role in Christian development at many different levels. It's time for believers to embrace the marketplace as an engine of revival and personal transformation.

> **It's time for believers to embrace the marketplace as an engine of revival and personal transformation**

As we do, Marketplace Christians will discover they have a calling to ministry that's just as significant as any other calling spoken of in the Bible. We'll discuss several of those callings in the next chapter.

CHAPTER 3

six kingdom callings

There is an enormous amount of teaching these days on the
five-fold ministry of the apostles, prophets, evangelists,
pastors and teachers (Eph 4:11). Much of the teaching
pertains to the restoration of these ministries to the church, but this
teaching, while important, often leaves Marketplace Christians
scratching their heads and wondering where they fit in the five-
fold schematic. Many conclude they don't fit at all, and many
question whether or not God knew what He was doing when He
made them with their particular talents.

The good news for Marketplace Christians is that the five-fold
ministries are only a handful of the millions of valid callings in the
heart of God. From a business perspective, I have observed six
distinct Kingdom callings which are modeled in scripture and
which directly relate to the giftings and callings of Marketplace
Christians.

The Corneliuses

Cornelius was a devout, God-fearing man who touched the heart of God with his prayers and giving. He was also the first Gentile to hear the Gospel, and he became the bridge that brought the gospel to a foreign culture, the Gentiles. One of the most amazing statements ever spoken about a human being was spoken about Cornelius: "Your prayers and alms have ascended as a memorial before God." (Acts 10:4, NASB)

Because they carry with them the aroma of the presence of God, they greatly impact those around them

Present-day Corneliuses are "prayer and alms" people, called to work "as for the Lord," to give liberally and pray earnestly. By their faith and because they carry with them the aroma of the presence of God, they greatly impact those around them, acting as a sturdy bridge to bring the Gospel to those in the marketplace. Furthermore, Corneliuses have a special calling to tug at the heart of God with their simple devotion.

I know a "Cornelius" who moved his family to Kansas City to be a part of the International House of Prayer, the 24/7, 365-day-a-year prayer and worship ministry founded by Mike Bickle. This man works a full-time job, usually forty to fifty hours a week, and gives generously to the Lord. Most days, before and after work, he comes to the House of Prayer and prays with heartfelt emotion. Though he is a simple man, there is an aroma of devotion about him – and I believe he moves the heart of God.

The Craftsmen

Most students of the scriptures cannot name the first instance of someone being filled with the Spirit of God. They are surprised to find it in the building of the tabernacle of Moses:

¹Now the LORD spoke to Moses, saying, ²"See, I have called by name Bezalel, the son of Uri, the son of Hur, of the tribe of Judah. ³"I have filled him with the Spirit of God in wisdom, in understanding, in knowledge, and in all kinds of craftsmanship, ⁴to make artistic designs for work in gold, in silver, and in bronze, ⁵and in the cutting of stones for settings, and in the carving of wood, that he may work in all kinds of craftsmanship. ⁶"And behold, I Myself have appointed with him Oholiab, the son of Ahisamach, of the tribe of Dan; and in the hearts of all who are skillful I have put skill, that they may make all that I have commanded you:" Ex. 31:1-6 (NASB)

> **The first mention in scripture of anyone being filled with the Spirit of God speaks not of prophecy, nor miracles, but *craftsmanship***

The first mention in scripture of anyone being filled with the Spirit of God speaks not of prophecy, nor miracles, but *craftsmanship*! In Bezalel's case, God gave him supernatural ability and creativity to work with gold, silver, precious stones and wood. Modern craftsmen include engineers, artisans, analysts, accountants, lawyers — anyone dedicated to understanding the intricacies of their trade as well as blessing God and people through it. Accountants are craftsmen of numbers, writers craftsmen of words. You might be a craftsman of lawn care, sewing or auto repair. Each type of craftsman has a special revelation of the Creator God who lives to create and is interested in all of creation down to the minute details.

Is there such thing as an anointed accountant? One friend, a senior auditor with a "big-five" accounting firm has an amazingly close walk with God, and continually communes with God and prays as she works. One day during an audit, a certain number jumped out at her, and she knew there was something wrong. After much research she was unable to find anything amiss, but still was convinced. She communicated her suspicions with her boss. He pressed her for the source of her suspicions, and when she admitted it was God, he rolled his eyes and groaned. But he began to watch that area more closely. Sometime later, it was discovered there was massive fraud, related to the numbers she had found. Yes, there are "craftsmen of accounting!"

> Each type of craftsman has a special revelation of the Creator God who lives to create and is interested in all of creation down to the minute details

George Washington Carver was a poor, self-educated ex-slave who became enamored with the peanut, considered at that time to be little more than a weed. He asked God to show him what the peanut might be good for, since He had created it. Carver invented two hundred uses for the peanut and single-handedly transformed the impoverished economy of the post-Civil War South. To him, inventing was simply about the discovery God. Listen to his heart:

"Nature in its varied forms are the little windows through which God permits me to commune with him, and to see much of his glory, majesty and power by simply lifting the curtain and looking in."

He was a craftsman of agriculture.

I was trained as a computer engineer and considered myself a craftsman of code. I loved writing code to the glory of God. I wrote code that people said was impossible to do. I would sit for hours quietly before my computer and craft the very finest code. I fellowshipped with God, and at times we wrote together. Several times when I was stumped, I asked God to help me, and I had a dream that showed me where the problem was! I worked hard to improve my craft and become the best engineer possible, and as a result, wherever I went, I quickly became one of the top engineers in the company.

> The heart of a craftsman — to please God by giving Him the most creative and inspired work we can do

This desire for excellence spans the ages. I was reading a volume on the history of Byzantium when I came across a photograph of an ancient reliquary made of solid gold, intricately carved with figures and scriptures. Monks, working mostly with hand-tools, had made it nearly 1,500 years ago. It was stunningly beautiful and clearly represented years of loving labor by many monks. Then I read the caption: "The reliquary was to never leave the inner sanctuary of the church, and was *never to be seen by the eyes of man.*" These monks had spent good portions of their lives to produce something of overwhelming value and beauty, only for their Creator! They had the heart of a craftsman — to please God by giving Him the most creative and inspired work we can do.

In London there is a shoemaker named only Lobb which has been in business for hundreds of years. Lobb has no sign on its door and has never advertised. Yet it has made shoes for nearly every king of England and thousands of celebrities for hundreds of years. Lobb's shoes cost $5,000 a pair and take nine months or more to make. But customers say once you wear a pair you can never go back. Their craftsmen make wooden carvings of your feet, and then build the shoe around the carving. Of Lobb the scripture is true:

[29]Do you see a man skilled in his work? He will stand before kings; He will not stand before obscure men. Prov. 22:29 (NASB)

God is the ultimate craftsman! He loves creating beauty, and He loves sharing His creative gift with earthly craftsmen. Marketplace Christians with the craftsmen calling are motivated to craft for Him, to give Him the very best, and in the process they receive and reflect a unique revelation of the Creator God.

The Governors

"Governors" have gifts of government, or "administrations," as it is called in 1 Cor. 12:28. They are called to rule the affairs of businesses, churches and ministries, and civil governments, and they often have an extraordinary revelation of the Ruler God. Joseph, Moses, David, Solomon, Daniel and Nehemiah are biblical examples of governors.

Whatever governors govern, works better. Joseph, though a slave, was promoted over all the affairs of Potiphar's house and Potiphar greatly prospered. When he worked for Pharaoh, Joseph again rose quickly to leadership, and Pharaoh prospered because Joseph was gifted as a governor.

There are many governors in business today. The world's most effective leaders operate in this God-given governmental gifting, even if they don't serve God. "For the gifts and the calling of God are irrevocable." (Rom. 11:29). Marketplace Christian Mike Frank is a present-day governor. Whatever he touches comes into order and prospers. He has served in the executive ranks of General Mills, Pepsico, Disney and Level (3) Communications. He was rapidly promoted in each company and his leadership helped bring them prosperity. Often when he left, the company began struggling. Mike also helped lead the International House of Prayer, and his "governorship" there had similar results.

> **If the church is to play any kind of leadership role in the world, it must be led by powerfully anointed governors**

Governors sometimes face opposition from insecure, ego-driven people who feel threatened by their extraordinary gift. Joseph's brothers sold him into slavery. Potiphar and Pharaoh, on the other hand, rightly saw Joseph as the goose that laid the golden eggs. The question for the church today is, what will it do with its governors? Will it feel threatened? Or will it recognize and value burgeoning governors and encourage them to fully embrace their calling? If the church is to play any kind of leadership role in the world, it must be led by powerfully anointed governors who rule from a heart passionate for God.

Treasure Bringers

Treasure bringers are anointed by God to make money and to do great deeds of compassion and mercy for the nations. They are spiritual Robin Hoods, and their joy is in plundering the wealth of the world for their Lord. They are entirely motivated by a revelation of the benevolent God and are completely free from the spirit of mammon.

They are entirely motivated by a revelation of the benevolent God

They have a righteous love of money, because they know what money can be used for. Of necessity they are the humblest of men and women, free from the control spirit and never seeking their own glory.

Treasure bringers are described in Isaiah 60:11:

[11] Your gates will be open continually;
They will not be closed day or night,
So that men may bring to you the wealth of the nations,
With their kings led in procession.
Isa. 60:11 (NASB)

That chapter of Isaiah foretells great darkness in the earth, the emergence of the mature glorified church (the Bride of Christ) and the wealth of the nations coming to her. Treasure bringers are those anointed by God to facilitate this massive wealth-transfer.

Gary Ginter is a present-day treasure bringer. As he was on the verge of becoming a missionary, God spoke to him to go into the marketplace. Gary founded the Chicago Research & Trading Group which became a moneymaking sensation. The Wall Street Journal dubbed it "the envy of the industry." Gary and his wife are worth multiple millions, yet they live in a modest 3-bedroom house and drive old cars. They have given millions to missions. Gary once said, "God has called me to make all the money I can, but live on as little as possible and give the rest away."

The Ginters' example illustrate how God is establishing a new ethos of "financial eunuchs." A eunuch in former days was one who was *trusted because of lack of personal desire.* Financial eunuchs will have little personal desire for wealth, and will have God's trust. Many will "live within a circle," only taking what they need, so they can give more to the Lord.

> **Joseph, for instance, *controlled* the land, grain and riches of Pharaoh, but *owned* none of it**

Many treasure bringers will not actually *own* the wealth they manage. Joseph, for instance, *controlled* the land, grain and riches of Pharaoh, but *owned* none of it. This is a strategy God uses to keep the hearts of His treasure bringers pure. Yet Joseph was still able to provide for God's people and build a city for them, Goshen.

One present-day treasure bringer had a dream similar to what Isaiah described (above). In the dream, there was a castle on a mountain, and seated on the throne was Jesus. Kings were lined up before Him, the line running down the great hall, out the door and all the way down the mountain. Each king had arms full of treasure. They were filled with joy as they laid their treasure at Jesus' feet, then ran back as fast as they could to get more.

As the church grows into maturity, becoming like Jesus, we will see treasure bringers come forth in increasing measure. God will use their extraordinary generosity to finance anointed ministries, help the needy, perform miracles of compassion on a national scale and build "cities of habitation" (we'll discuss those in a minute).

Marketplace Redeemers

I wrote earlier of spiritual oases of ministry and Kingdom life that will spring up within workplaces. Marketplace redeemers are the ones who build these oases. They don't look primarily to church meetings for their spheres of spiritual activity, but build the Kingdom of God where they are, establishing the presence of God in the marketplace. They have a revelation of the God of all of life, the God whose glory will fill the whole earth (Numbers 14:21). They will usher in the great harvest "outside the camp."

> Often, marketplace redeemers have a marketplace calling, but are **loaded with ministry giftings as well**

Often, marketplace redeemers have a marketplace calling, but are loaded with ministry giftings as well. For years I was confused because I was good at engineering and business, but also loved teaching and pastoring people. I had ministry giftings, but didn't understand they were to function within the marketplace.

Rick Joyner has said that over 90% of God's pastors are in the marketplace – because that's where the people are. The same goes for apostles, prophets, evangelists, and teachers.

Marketplace redeemers must realize they are not called to vocational ministry, but to the marketplace. Some will build anointed businesses. Others will build spiritual oases in the midst of world systems in education, business, the military and civil government. Stay-at-home moms and dads are also marketplace redeemers who establish the oases of the presence of God where they are. Wherever they find themselves, marketplace redeemers use their sphere of authority to build these oases which are characterized by the presence of God, joy, love for others and ministry to the saved and unsaved alike.

> **Over 90% of God's pastors are in the marketplace – because that's where the people are. The same goes for apostles, prophets, evangelists, and teachers.**

City Builders

One of God's strategies for bringing mercy in the midst of dark times is to build "cities of habitation," places of refuge from the storms of life and the rage of the enemy. Cities of habitation are described in detail in Psalm 107. City builders — the "architects" of these cities — have a strong anointing to build, combined with a strong patriarchal or matriarchal anointing. They are motivated and empowered by a revelation of the patriarchal God and the Protector God. They also are terrific networkers of people and institutions.

Joseph was a city builder who built Goshen, which became a city of habitation. While everyone else endured the great famine, those in Goshen were fed from the table of the King. During the great plagues and judgments that came under Moses, Goshen was protected. In Goshen, the Israelites grew from a family of seventy-five Bedouin nomads into a great nation. They developed their own economy, local government, community, education, culture, art and more.

Nehemiah was another city builder. He literally rebuilt the city walls and established a strong government. He also modeled the ability to network, bringing together people and resources for an anointed purpose. As city builders emerge within the church, they will bring people together from the other five callings — leaders, craftsmen, Corneliuses, marketplace redeemers and treasure bringers. I imagine a day when city builders will unite health care leaders, city planners, ministry leaders, school teachers, mothers, fathers, business owners and public servants, all to serve God by achieving a particular goal. The effect will be strong cities, places of refuge and compassion where God's mercy is expressed to people.

These six Kingdom callings form the heart of marketplace Christianity. As the church encourages and embraces these callings, along with the five-fold ministry and the many other callings God gives people, the results will be extraordinary and unprecedented.

One of these callings — leadership — is so critical that it deserves a chapter of its own.

CHAPTER 4

the leadership gifts

Why do the best businesses run like German automobiles, while others sputter along, never getting out of first gear? Why do some ministries, like Bill Bright's Campus Crusade for Christ, become models of vision, organization and efficiency while others repeatedly fail, no matter how much money they are given?

The answer is leadership. Leadership consultant Les Woller defines leaders as those who "create meaning so that others can think and act." Leaders are usually visionaries who articulate their vision, recruit well, think strategically, initiate change, disrupt the continuum and create chaos.

As we saw before, managers are leaders' critical counterparts. They turn chaos into order, put the right people in the right roles and clearly define goals, roles and boundaries. They design systems and processes that bring out each person's best, causing him or her to perform at a higher level than he or she otherwise would. Managers maximize efficiency so activity produces results and no resources are wasted. Leaders define the "why," managers define the "how." Leaders without managers create lots of vision and activity, but frustration and fruitlessness. Managers without leaders create order and peace, but without purpose, and ultimately a different kind of frustration and fruitlessness. It takes leaders *and* managers to produce good government, and the peace, fruitfulness and sense of meaning that come with it.

The apostle Paul was well aware of the importance of leadership. In listing the well-known ministry gifts, he also mentions something he calls "administrations:"

[28]And God has appointed in the church, first apostles, second prophets, third teachers, then miracles, then gifts of healings, helps, administrations, various kinds of tongues. 1 Corinthians 12:28 (NASB)

Most casual readers assume "administrations" refers to secretaries and office managers. But Paul already mentioned those gifts under the title of "helps." The word *administration* actually means *to govern*. Why don't we hear more about the gift of administration? I don't know, but I can say with confidence I've never heard a sermon about it in my entire Christian experience. We ignore the leadership gifts at our peril, and we must take them just as seriously as we take the spiritual gifts and the ministry gifts. Each gift is critical to the church's success.

Where are the Leaders?

At critical periods in church history, God has raised up people with extraordinary gifts of government: Joseph, Moses, David, Solomon and Nehemiah. Today, God is also raising up many thousands with gifts of government, and equipping them with the tools of leadership. This calling is critical if the church is to be properly led through the challenges of the next millennium.

George Barna is a well-known church pollster. For years he was troubled that the church did not seem particularly effective or relevant. His mission became to equip church leaders with information and understanding to better reach the nation with the gospel. He founded Barna Research and for ten years gathered information about the faith and beliefs of Americans. He detailed and quantified where Americans place themselves in their faith and their relationship with church. But recently, Barna announced that after ten years, he had failed in his mission. He said he'd assumed the church was failing because it lacked the information it needed; but after 10 years, he believes the problem is not a lack of *information*, but a lack of *leadership* – the real problem was that church leaders were generally not true leaders.

> **For the church to become strong again, we must heed the guidance of the leaders God has called and gifted for that purpose**

"The people who fill the positions of leadership in churches today are, for the most part, teachers—good people, lovers of God, well-educated, gifted communicators – but not leaders," Barna wrote.

"They do not have or understand vision. They are incapable of motivating and mobilizing people around God's vision. They fail to direct people's energies and resources effectively and efficiently. For the church to become strong again, we must heed the guidance of the leaders God has called and gifted for that purpose, while growing through the focused teaching of those who are gifted to explicate his Word and its profound implications for our lives."

While there are many exceptions, I agree with Barna that as a whole, the modern church has not created nor attracted strong leaders. Meanwhile, the marketplace attracts and produces leaders by the truckload. Gifted leaders gravitate to opportunity, challenge and learning environments offered by businesses. They are repelled by the small vision, autocratic leadership, lack of objectivity, chaos and foolishness that characterize many church environments. The best leaders avoid the political arena as well because of its small-mindedness, blind ambition, dishonesty and inability to address real issues. In church and politics, there is often little recognition or reward for effective leadership. But in business, leaders find their natural environment. They are almost always welcomed, rewarded, groomed and given opportunity. Jesus spoke about this phenomenon in the parable of the minas, where those who managed *business* well were given *cities* to rule:

> **Jesus tied the governance anointing to business. He recognized that leadership is produced in the marketplace**

[12]So He said, "A nobleman went to a distant country to receive a kingdom for himself, and then return. [13]"And he called ten of his slaves, and gave them ten minas and said to them, 'Do business with this until I come back.' ... [17]"And he said to him, 'Well done, good slave, because you have been faithful in a very little thing, you are to be in authority over ten cities.' Luke 19:12-13, 17 (NASB)

Jesus tied the governance anointing to business. He recognized that leadership is produced in the marketplace, and He made *the marketplace* — not vocational ministry — the primary arena where the leaders of His millennial kingdom will receive their "training for reigning."

Marketplace Leaders and the Church

There ought to be a symbiotic relationship between business leaders and the church. Business leaders should enable and empower the church with their gifts. The church should help

There ought to be a symbiotic relationship between business leaders and the church

leaders understand and wholeheartedly pursue their purpose in life. There should be healthy overlap between the marketplace and the church, each supplementing and breathing life into the other. Yet the church often doesn't know what to do with its business leaders. They sit in the pews like priceless, untapped resources. If churches knew how to draw out that resource, they'd discover that strong leadership exhibits and produces vision, unity of purpose and selflessness.

Weak leadership does the opposite. Because of weak leadership, hundreds of denominations and thousands of independent churches tend to their separate kingdoms. Church leaders can be gripped by insecurity, selfish ambition, suspicion, competition and control. They sometimes care more about growing their numbers, having a seat of honor and having money than they care about their sheep. Churches are crippled by disagreement, disunity and infighting. It reminds me of medieval history, when a king would die and false leaders would rise up and fight for power. Or like recent examples in Somalia, Haiti and elsewhere where the central government collapsed and competing warlords vied for control. Good leadership — think of Abraham Lincoln, George Washington, Martin Luther King, Jr., King David, Moses, William Wallace, Charlemagne and many others — creates unity of heart and purpose. Poor leadership has disastrous results.

This is also true of management. If there is growth without good management, there will be an even faster-growing chaos that undermines the growth. I have worked with many organizations that lacked management skill — including my own business at times. Though the businesses grew, they hit growth plateaus. The larger they grew, the more chaos was created. As chaos multiplied it undermined the growth, and more energy was spent fighting fires as the infrastructure collapsed because of poor management. Too many churches lack effective management. As a result, resources are squandered; there is little fruit despite a surplus of programs and activity, and all the growth leads to disunity and collapse.

Some church leaders already realize the importance of bringing in leaders who've been refined in the marketplace. One prominent ministry leader brought two senior businessmen into senior leadership. Though he has led ministries for twenty-five years, he was amazed at the impact they had. "They are the two best leaders I have ever worked with," he said. "There is no way we would be where we are as a ministry without them."

Bill Bright, founder of Campus Crusade for Christ, built a huge, excellent organization that empowered thousands of people and ran like a well-oiled machine. Bill told Mike Bickle, "The best decision I ever made was to get entrepreneurial leadership in place and get out of the way."

> **Bill told Mike Bickle, "The best decision I ever made was to get entrepreneurial leadership in place and get out of the way."**

Bickle followed suit, bringing key business leaders into core leadership roles at the International House of Prayer. By all counts, they revolutionized the ministry.

For Pastors

So what is the role of church? What part are pastors to play in the emergence of Marketplace Christianity?

The Church is God's primary institution in the earth. It is to be a place of encounter with God and equipping of the saints. But it is *not to be the primary place of spiritual expression or ministry.*

By defining church programs and meetings as the primary arena of spiritual activity, operation of our spiritual gifts, and fulfillment of our spiritual calling, a great dislocation has ensued.

First, it creates great pressure and even wars inside the walls of church. Marketplace leaders were born to conquer, to rule, and to lead. But if the walls of church are defined as their primary arena of function, then they will vie for validation, voice, authority, position, and honor within church – a place they were never designed to function in a primary way. It is like locking a hundred generals in a room and telling them this room is where they are to fulfill their destiny.

Second, the "great army" of God, the 97% of believers who are not called to vocational ministry, become dormant and disengaged from church. This is not because they do not want to serve, or because they are self-centered, or unspiritual. It is because the roles defined for them inside the walls of church just don't quite fit who they are. The more they feel pressured to do so the more conflicted they become, though few can even articulate what they are feeling or why they are reluctant.

> **The roles defined for them inside the walls of church just don't quite fit who they are**

Third, the marketplace revival God has ordained doesn't happen. As Billy Graham has stated, "I believe one of the next great moves of God is going to be through the believers in the workplace." But if those who are to usher in the revival are disengaged from their primary field of ministry, it remains a spiritual desert

Marketplace Christians are to be a nation of priests to the marketplace. As 1 Pet. 2:9 teaches, "But you are a chosen people, a royal priesthood, a holy nation." We are a *royal* priesthood – that is a *kingly* priesthood, ruling in the affairs of life. Pastors and vocational ministers are to be priests to this royal priesthood – not in the sense of being intermediaries, but equippers.

The current model of church ministry revolves primarily around getting people involved in church meetings and programs. But thousands of churches are embracing new models emphasizing equipping Marketplace Christians to be fruitful where they are.

97% of the pastoral, evangelistic, teaching, prophetic, and apostolic gifts are in Marketplace Christians and are to primarily operate in the marketplace. For Marketplace Christians, their field is their workplace, and their flock is the people they work with. *The main function of the 5-fold ministries is to equip Marketplace Christians for works of service in their field of ministry* – which is where God has placed them in the marketplace:

> **For Marketplace Christians, their field is their workplace, and their flock is the people they work with**

[11]And He gave some as apostles, and some as prophets, and some as evangelists, and some as pastors and teachers, [12]for the equipping of the saints for the work of service, to the building up of the body of Christ; [13]until we all attain to the unity of the faith, and of the knowledge of the Son of God, to a mature man, to the measure of the stature which belongs to the fullness of Christ. Ephesians 4:11-13 (NASB)

If God were ever to call me into being a pastor again, I would do one key thing very differently: instead of spending the bulk of my time responding to the needs and demands of my congregation, I would find the 20% of my congregation who were already fruitful in the marketplace and spend 80% of my energy and focus with them, helping equip them to be even more fruitful where they are.

Every Marketplace Christian I have met is desperate for equipping to be more effective for God where they are.

When the revival was happening in my business, I was mostly clueless about how to steward it, and I did not do a very good job. If a minister had come alongside me and prayed with me, and helped me figure out how to steward it, foster it, and help it grow, I would have been greatly blessed, and the revival would have undoubtedly been many times greater.

Every Marketplace Christian I have met is desperate for equipping to be more effective for God where they are. Among other things, they want to know (1) how to share the gospel in a normal, natural way; (2) how to pray for and minister to people; (3) how to walk in intimacy with God throughout their day; (4) how to hear God and be effectively "led by the Spirit" in their day.

Here are a few other ways pastors and church leaders can become marketplace-friendly:

1. Publicly acknowledge Marketplace Christians – *give them value* – for something besides their giving money and time to church programs. Ask them what God is doing in their marketplace. Have

them give regular public testimonies of what God is doing in their marketplace.

At all of our conferences, we always have a Marketplace Christian Luncheon. At their tables, we ask them each to tell what they do, then tell "what God is doing in their marketplace." Then I have them testify. It is always stunning. Many, for the first time, realize that God is moving in their life. Many, for the first time, realize they have, or can have an affective ministry. Many, for the first time, feel valued. And hearing their peers, their eyes are opened to the possibilities, and their faith soars.

2. Publicly bless Marketplace Christians. This can be one of the most powerful things you can do, yet is sadly overlooked by most ministers. Aaron and the priests were commanded to bless the people:

23 *Speak to Aaron and to his sons, saying, 'Thus you shall bless the sons of Israel. You shall say to them:*
24 *The LORD bless you, and keep you;*
25 *The LORD make His face shine on you, And be gracious to you;*
26 *The LORD lift up His countenance on you, And give you peace.'*
27 *So they shall invoke My name on the sons of Israel, and I then will bless them.*
Numbers 6:23-27 (NASB)

Marketplace Christians *covet* this. By blessing them you are communicating that they are valuable, and that both you and God are deeply committed to them, and that you are backing them up and cheerleading for them.

3. Start a prayer meeting for Marketplace Christians. We have a once-per-week prayer meeting specifically for Marketplace Christians. We worship, pray what we call "Nehemiah" prayers for the Kingdom of God to come to the marketplace, and then we have a time of personal prayer and ministry for everyone in the marketplace, praying for their individual needs: favor, a new boss, release of finances, wisdom, etc. Week after week, I have been told with tears of gratitude, "I can't believe this! I I feel so blessed that you all are standing with me for my needs!"

Churches and business leaders must rediscover each other; they must open their eyes to the mutual benefits of a strong relationship, and begin working together to establish the Kingdom in the marketplace and in the sanctuary. As they do, there will be an explosion of well-managed growth and vision that turns the church, and the world, upside down.

CHAPTER 5

what to love about money

One of the main misunderstandings about the marketplace is that it's all about money. Christians have a sneaking suspicion that money is dirty and sinful; that it ought to be handled infrequently and with gloves on. They think they're quoting the Bible when they say, "Money is the root of all evil." In fact, the Bible says, "*Love* of money is the root of all *kinds* of evil" (1 Tim. 6:10). Too many people think "Marketplace Christian" is the same as "carnal Christian" — an excuse to glorify money while giving it a thin, biblical veneer.

In fact, money is neither good nor evil. It's a morally neutral tool, an ingenious invention that allows for efficiency in markets. Money only becomes evil when our hearts wrongly attach to it, as the scripture above indicates. To fully appreciate marketplace Christianity, every believer must understand money from a truly biblical perspective. They must see it as a tool given by God, something to be used but not glorified, appreciated but not elevated. They must understand how it derives its value, and how it is best used.

Appreciating Money

Money has two basic functions, the first being to help markets run efficiently. If the world had only two people, a sheepherder and a wheat farmer, money would not be needed. They would simply trade between themselves at an agreed exchange rate of wheat per sheep. This rate would fluctuate depending on the relative supply

Money is the right to the goods and services of others

and demand of both commodities. But add a cow herder, a vegetable farmer, a carpenter, a blacksmith and a clothing maker, and suddenly there are simply too many exchange rates to keep track of. Money simplifies those exchanges – every commodity has a single exchange rate: to money – which is its price. This greatly simplifies exchange and creates an efficient market.

Money's second purpose is to store value. If a farmer sells all his excess wheat, but doesn't immediately need to buy sheep, he can "store" the proceeds from his harvest as money, which is far less perishable.

Why Money is Valuable

Money is not to be *coveted*, but is to be deeply *appreciated* for what it represents – the combined labor and love of a chain of servants. A friend of mine once visited a coffee-processing factory. As the proprietor was giving a group of investors a tour, he discovered a lone coffee bean on the floor. He picked up the bean, carefully washed it off, and returned it to its bin. One of the investors chided him for wasting his time with one bean when there were millions more. The proprietor replied, "If you knew what went into that bean, you would do the same."

When I heard that story, I thought about what went into producing that bean. I thought of the mountainside in the jungles in Colombia where God made a special place that grows the best coffee in the world. I thought about the farmer who cared for and groomed the coffee plants and protected them from pests, who carefully and lovingly handpicked every bean from the tree at just the right time and who carried them down the mountain and laid them in rows to dry. I thought about the farmer's grandfather, who cleared the land and selected the best coffee plants, carefully nurturing them and passing them on to his sons. I thought about the coffee buyer who learned the skill of selecting just the right beans to make the kind of brew he desired. I thought about the coffee bean roaster, the blend-master, the café owner, and the *barista* who all added their own unique and careful touch.

> Every coffee bean, every garment, every dollar put into an offering bucket represents the combined labor of a hundred servants

When you think of it that way, one coffee bean has much more valuable than would appear, and so does most every commodity. Every coffee bean, every garment, every dollar put into an offering bucket represents the combined labor of a hundred servants. It represents the forgone desires of some precious soul who could have done something else with his or her time and labor. As Christians we must see money for what it represents – an unbroken chain of love, leading back to the Father.

Wealth and Riches

The scriptures speak extensively of money, riches and wealth, three related but distinct concepts. My basic definition of money is this: Money is the right to the goods and services of others. I define riches as *an abundance of money and possessions.* Wealth is slightly different – it is the ability to create money by *controlling the means of production.* The Bible often associates wealth with land and flocks, which in a modern economy equates to *business*, which is the modern means of production. If money were *water*, then riches would be a *bucket* of water, and wealth a *river* of water. Or in terms of cash, riches are a *pile of cash*, and wealth is *cash flow*. Riches are limited and can be depleted by loss or consumption. Wealth, on the other hand, creates a steady flow of income.

Wealth is the ability to create riches by controlling the means of production

Abram had both riches and wealth, gold and silver and vast flocks and fields (Gen. 13:2). He may have come from a wealthy family, but undoubtedly most of his gold and silver was obtained in trade for his production.

Wealth is others-oriented. Abram's household supported more than three hundred trained men (Gen. 14:14), and probably a far larger number when women and children are included. These were his "employees" who worked the fields and tended the flocks, and were provided for in return.

> **Wealth gives us the ability to provide for others without depleting our resources**

Wealth gives us the ability to provide for others without depleting our resources. For example, if a needy family had arrived on Abram's doorstep, he could have taken care of them by putting them to work in his fields. But instead of costing Abram, they would have actually *expanded* his production capabilities.

Wealth also gives us the ability to create a spiritual oasis. Abram likely hired into his household many refugees seeking to escape the depravity of nearby Sodom and Gomorrah. In Abram's house they would have found a functioning marketplace *and* a spiritual oasis. This is why I encourage people to start or buy businesses. By owning a business, we control the means of production and create wealth; we can hire good people, and provide for them; we can care for customers by producing goods and services for them; and we can create spiritual oases amongst our employees.

Wealth is a Blessing from God

All wealth comes from God and belongs to God:

¹⁰ *For every beast of the forest is Mine,*
    The cattle on a thousand hills.
Psa. 50:10 (NASB)

Christians should get rid of the idea that wealth equals carnality. The Bible is full of very wealthy believers — Abraham, Isaac, Jacob, Joseph, Moses, Job, David and Solomon, to name just a few. The scriptures are clear that wealth is a blessing from God:

²² *It is the blessing of the LORD that makes rich,*
    And He adds no sorrow to it.
Prov. 10:22 (NASB)

The scriptures are clear that wealth is a blessing from God

¹² *Now Isaac sowed in that land and reaped in the same year a hundredfold. <u>And the LORD blessed him,</u> ¹³<u>and the man became rich,</u> and continued to grow richer until he became very wealthy; ¹⁴for he had possessions of flocks and herds and a great household, so that the Philistines envied him. Gen. 26:12-14 (NASB)*

¹ *Praise the LORD!*
    How blessed is the man who fears the LORD,
    Who greatly delights in His commandments.
² *His descendants will be mighty on earth;*
    <u>The generation of the upright will be blessed.</u>
³ *<u>Wealth and riches are in his house,</u>*
    And his righteousness endures forever.
Psa. 112:1-3 (NASB)

When God established the covenant with Abraham, He promised He would bless him and make him a great nation. Several hundred years later, God spoke to Moses, saying He was going to bless the Israelites and give them "the power to make wealth," *because of the Abrahamic Covenant*:

[18] "But you shall remember the LORD your God, for it is He who is giving you power to make wealth, that He may confirm His covenant which He swore to your fathers, as it is this day. Deut. 8:18 (NASB)

God is committed to giving His people the power to make wealth, not just for our sakes, but to fulfill the promise made to Abraham. He *must* bless His people to confirm His covenant with Abraham.

Creating Value

All wealth comes from *creating value*: Creating value is simply creating something that:

All wealth comes from *creating value*

1) never existed before, and

2) which has value to someone else.

Growing a cucumber, fixing a car, cleaning a house, babysitting, and building a home are all ways of creating value. Every normal human being has the capability to create value in some way. Creating value is simply *serving*. I am always amazed by people who are idle but complain about not having money. I want to tell them, "You have two hands...you have a brain...go *do* something for someone!" Serving always creates value, and money naturally follows value. It's a simple, logical flow.

In creating value, we have the opportunity to be like God, who is always *creating for others*. In so doing, we earn the right to receive some value in return. This is how people "care" for one another. If no one ever created value, no one would have anything to eat, have a place to sleep, or clothes to wear. Paul touched on this principle in Ephesians 4:28:

If no one ever created value, no one would have anything to eat, have a place to sleep, or clothes to wear

[28]He who steals must steal no longer; but rather he must labor, performing with his own hands what is good, so that he will have something to share with one who has need. (NASB)

Many people are gripped by a *scarcity mentality* which says since there is only so much food, clothing and other goods to go around, adding a new person means less for everyone. But this is flawed, ungodly thinking. Each new person brings needs, but also brings the ability to create value for others. For example, when a family joined Abram's household, he fed them, but they actually expanded his productivity by adding new abilities to his "marketplace." Envy is rooted in the scarcity mentality. Envy compares what *you* have to what *they* have, and it fails to grasp that every human being has the ability to create *unlimited* value, according to his skill and creativity.

A business is nothing more than a value-creation organization. Each employee uses his or her special skills to create value for customers. A ministry, too, is a value-creation organization, creating value for its members and for those it serves. God's divine order dictates that if we stop creating value as an organization, we forfeit our right to exist. This is good, since businesses that don't create value are tying up resources but not serving others. It's better for those resources to go to a business that does create value. Likewise, churches that do not create value will fail, freeing up resources for churches that create value.

We can create even more value by enhancing our skills. This option is open to anyone in any field. Going to school for training and education will enable you to serve better. An entrepreneur who goes to business school will have more tools and skills to create value than one who doesn't. A young man who apprentices himself to a master mechanic will pick up skills in a few months that might otherwise have taken years to learn. Each of us should constantly hunt for new skills to add to our value-creation toolbox.

> **God's divine order dictates that if we stop creating value as an organization, we forfeit our right to exist**

Lee Iacocca is a good example of this. In the 1980s, Chrysler Corporation was on the verge of failure. Iacocca came in and turned the company around, creating billions of dollars in value for the tens of thousands of employees who would have lost their jobs, as well as the thousands of shareholders who would have lost their savings. He was only able to pull off this business "miracle" because he had spent time learning skills throughout his career, and therefore he had more power to create value.

Another way to create value is by being creative. In the 1800s the seeds were removed from cotton by a laborious manual process. Then Eli Whitney invented the cotton gin, a device that could remove the seeds automatically. Overnight, the work of a hundred people could be done by three people. With one idea, Whitney reduced the cost of cotton production by 97 percent, creating *billions* of dollars in value for cotton farmers and for clothing buyers who would pay less for cotton clothing.

The Poverty Spirit

I spent many years in poor areas of Los Angeles and many hours working with people who had grown up in impoverished circumstances. I was continually surprised by the poor choices they made. Some couldn't consistently buy groceries, yet drove elaborately fixed-up automobiles, gambled at the casinos, spent $200 on a pair of sneakers, $50 a month on lottery tickets and $200 a month on cigarettes. These same people viewed money as the solution to every problem; they bought on impulse, were focused on consumption and took great pride in fancy cars, boats, clothing and jewelry. They completely overextended themselves with debt and yet openly disdained the creditors who took a risk on them. They were in chronic financial crisis because of mismanagement, and yet they considered "work" a dirty word.

I call this poison mentality *the poverty spirit*. Jesus called it the spirit of mammon (Matt. 6:24). The poverty spirit tells people to *pursue money apart from creating value*. Gambling, the lottery and theft are efforts to make money without creating value. When we pursue money apart from creating value for others, *we claim the right to the goods and services of others, but without offering any goods or services in return* – it is taking without giving in return. Paul spoke of the poverty spirit:

⁹But those who want to get rich fall into temptation and a snare and many foolish and harmful desires which plunge men into ruin and destruction. ¹⁰For the love of money is a root of all sorts of evil, and some by longing for it have wandered away from the faith and pierced themselves with many griefs. 1 Tim. 6:9-10 (NASB)

> **The poverty spirit tells people to pursue money apart from creating value**

The poverty spirit conspires to trap people in a cycle of poor choices and slavery to money. But it doesn't only afflict poor people. It afflicts the human heart and produces poverty. I have seen very wealthy people with it. Lottery winners, professional athletes and others who come into riches often end up impoverished. As scripture says,

²¹ An inheritance gained hurriedly at the beginning
  Will not be blessed in the end.
Prov. 20:21 (NASB)

By acting under the poverty spirit, we will "pierce ourselves with many griefs." Some pierce themselves with pyramid marketing schemes which masquerade as legitimate businesses. They prey on those with the poverty spirit – they promise riches without effort. Amazingly, such schemes find their most fertile ground in the church. Christians seem to think that God will give them money without our having to create value.

Breaking the spirit of poverty is simple: we must stop trying to get something for nothing, and instead create value for other people. The scriptures state it like this:

[28]*He who steals must steal no longer; but rather he must labor, performing with his own hands what is good, so that he will have something to share with one who has need. Eph. 4:28 (NASB)*

Breaking the spirit of poverty is simple: we must stop trying to get something for nothing, and instead create value for other people

I grew up in a family that was dirt-poor, but the poverty spirit did not rule us. My parents taught me the value of hard work; I learned that through work we could achieve high goals. Work breaks the poverty spirit. It opens our eyes to God's ordained system of productivity. It teaches us to create value for others, to become producers instead of consumers. It gives us the legitimate right to the goods and services of others. No government or charitable program can succeed unless the spirit of poverty is broken.

Two Views of Money

There are two views of money: the consumer view and the producer view. The consumer sees money simply as the means to consume. He sees work as a necessary evil. All children have the consumer view. When my young children got a dollar, their eyes filled with thoughts of candy and dime store junk they could buy. The consumer looks at opportunities and at others with a purely selfish perspective: "How can I benefit?"

The producer sees money as a reward for production and serving. Money is a byproduct of serving others. The producer looks at opportunities and at others and says, "How can I serve them?" The consumer looks to take while the producer to give.

> **The producer sees money as a reward for production and serving. Money is a byproduct of serving others**

Every father and mother must take on the producer view to some degree. As I earn money, I rarely think of the consumption items I can buy, but rather of the needs I can meet in my family and elsewhere.

The Entrepreneurial Spirit vs. the Exploitational Spirit

I have had the privilege of rubbing shoulders with some of the best entrepreneurs in the world. Many people believe entrepreneurs are greed-motivated, but that is patently untrue. The most successful entrepreneurs are not driven by greed but by passion for finding and solving the greatest needs. When I teach classes on entrepreneurialism I am often asked how to find a great moneymaking idea. I put it like this: "Find the most *people* in the most *pain*, and solve their *problem*." The essence of the entrepreneurial spirit is meeting others' needs.

The opposite of the entrepreneurial spirit is the exploitational spirit which is more concerned with getting money from a customer (or congregation member) than providing value. People (or businesses, or churches) with the exploitational spirit pursue riches by *using* a customer to enrich themselves, instead of *serving* the customer. *A customer is a checkbook.* For example, it seems whenever I rent a video at my local video store, I end up paying more in late fees than it would cost me to buy the videos! I imagine they have an army of analysts in a windowless room somewhere who pour over spreadsheets trying to figure out how to get more money out of their customers and give less in return. They have mastered the art of putting their hand in my pocket and extracting money.

> **The most successful entrepreneurs are not driven by greed but by passion for finding and solving the greatest needs**

An entrepreneur had a similar video store experience, but he decided to do something about it, so he started a company called NetFlix. With NetFlix, late fees don't exist. Customers pay $20 a month and watch as many videos as they want. They choose their movies online. The movies come in the mail and each movie comes with a return mailer. When they are finished with it, they just drop it in the mailbox, and the next video on their list automatically comes in the mail. NetFlix has become a Wall Street sensation: in just a few years they have over a million subscribers and a high-flying stock. This is an example of the entrepreneurial spirit overcoming the exploitational spirit.

Businesses with the exploitational spirit can have strong results in the short term, but in the long term they fail or are forced to change. Almost all great companies were founded with an entrepreneurial spirit, but over time became dominated by an exploitational spirit as the founders' passion was gradually supplanted by "professionals" with the desire to boost short-term results.

> **Businesses with the exploitational spirit can have strong results in the short term, but in the long term they fail or are forced to change**

When Christians ask my advice about starting a business, they often say they want to do it part time, so they can spend most of their time doing other stuff, which is what they really want to do. They see business as a vehicle to fund their true desire. Almost without exception, the conversation begins with money and why they need it. This is the exploitational spirit – it sees business primarily as a means of cashing a check and customers as a checkbook. Such people disrespect what I call the "sanctity of business" which is this:

Business is primarily about serving others, creating value, constantly improving products and services, committing to customers, being there for customers and supporting them long-term. It cannot be successful without intense passion and focus.

The exploitational spirit, on the other hand, tries to make as much money as possible and give as little as possible in return. This approach is doomed, as the Bible says:

[20] *A faithful man will abound with blessings,*

But he who makes haste to be rich will not go unpunished.
Prov. 28:20 (NASB)

[22] *A man with an evil eye hastens after wealth*
   And does not know that want will come upon him.
Prov. 28:22 (NASB)

Entrepreneurs who are committed to customers and passionate about serving them will always drive exploiters out of business. And for people who see business as a way to fund a different passion, I say, don't waste your life on something that is not your passion. Passion is God's voice in your heart, speaking to you about your calling. Psalm 37:4 says if we "delight ourselves in the Lord" that He will "give us the desires of our heart." He will literally fill our hearts with His desires for us. It is best to pursue our true passion and look for God's provision in it. To pursue our passion is to serve God, who is the author of our passion. To do otherwise is to *serve money*:

Business is primarily about serving others

"No one can serve two masters. Either he will hate the one and love the other, or he will be devoted to the one and despise the other. You cannot serve both God and Money. Matt. 6:24 (NIV)

A Biblical Understanding of Work

Perhaps most important is to understand the biblical value of work. As I said, many people I grew up with considered "work" a four-letter word. Yet it's difficult, perhaps impossible, to grasp the value of money until you work. Over the years I have watched the concept of work help my children mature in their understanding of money. As a young girl, my daughter viewed a dollar as a means to buy a new "doodad." But today as a teenager, she earns money by providing child-care in a health club – a challenging job. Now when she considers her purchases, I can see her weighing her desire to have the item against the hours she spent working at the club. Money now represents her time and energy. Because of work, money has been transformed in her thinking from a *means of consumption* to a *means of exchange* – her time and energy for another's.

> It's difficult, perhaps impossible, to grasp the value of money until you work

For many, perhaps most people, the goal is to graduate from work. In high school I remember telling my friends I wanted to become a millionaire by the time I was 30, then hire someone to "take my ulcers" while I retired on a beach somewhere. But as I thought about it, I realized, what's the point of life without work? Idleness? Pursuit of pleasure? If you are not working, you are not creating value. And if you are not creating value, you are consuming value created by others. Today my goals have changed. I love work, because I love serving others. I plan on serving in whatever capacity I am able, for as long as I am able.

I'm convinced that Christians will never graduate from work. Though it is difficult to prove from the scriptures, I believe even in heaven we will all work – as teachers, librarians, ministers and so on – serving God and serving others. The closest biblical pattern we have is the Garden of Eden, which is a shadow of heavenly paradise. And in the Garden, there was work. We're told,

*"The LORD God took the man and put him in the Garden of Eden
to work it [tend it, cultivate it] and take care of it" Gen 2:15 (NIV
– amplification added)*

This was not hard, burdensome work, but a means to encounter
and have joyful fellowship with God.

Once Jesus returns to establish his millennial kingdom on earth,
and after that when Jesus establishes the new heavens and the new
earth, the saints in heaven will return to earth to rule and reign (1
Thes. 4:13-17, Rev. 20). There
will certainly be work:
rebuilding, serving, caring for
others, and governing. And
when the thousand years are
over, there will be a new

**Work is a means to
encounter and have joyful
fellowship with God**

heavens and a new earth, it will be more of the same (Rev. 21, Isa.
65:17-23). As believers, we had better get ready for work!

The Bible goes on to praise work at every turn:

⁴ *Poor is he who works with a negligent hand,
But the hand of the diligent makes rich.*
Prov. 10:4 (NASB)

¹⁷ *He who loves pleasure will become a poor man;
He who loves wine and oil will not become rich.*
Prov. 21:17 (NASB)

¹¹ *Wealth obtained by fraud dwindles,
But the one who gathers by labor increases it.*

Prov. 13:11 (NASB)

Many of Jesus' parables were about work:

the parable of the talents (Matt 25:14-30);

the parable of the minas (Luke 19:11-27);

the parable of the unrighteous steward (Luke 16:1-9);

the parable of the fig tree (Luke 13:6-9).

God Himself is a worker: Jesus described Himself and the Father as the Vinedresser and the Shepherd. He was a worker in Creation; The Cross is called a "work;" Jesus called His earthly ministry His "work;" in heaven, He does

God Himself is a worker

the daily "work" of intercession. Does God love His work? Of course! It's an on-going expression of His love for us.

We're told to follow that example and love each other and love God by working. Paul exhorted New Testament Christians:

[10]For even when we were with you, we used to give you this order: if anyone is not willing to work, then he is not to eat, either. [11]For we hear that some among you are leading an undisciplined life, doing no work at all, but acting like busybodies. [12]Now such persons we command and exhort in the Lord Jesus Christ to work in quiet fashion and eat their own bread. 2 Thes. 3:10-12 (NASB)

Paul objected strongly to believers who became consumers and not producers. God's divine order is for everyone to be givers, not takers. Until we learn that lesson, God will resist us, and poverty and lack will be our lot.

Ephesians 4:28 gives five beautiful truths about work:

28He who steals must steal no longer; but rather he must labor, performing with his own hands what is good, so that he will have something to share with one who has need.

1) work is pure, because at its core, work is serving others;

2) work is good and gives satisfaction of a job well-done;

3) work creates value;

Work was given by God to be the primary activity of man during our earthly journey

4) work is the foundation of giving;

5) giving is the expression of love.

Work was given by God to be the primary activity of man during our earthly journey. Through work, we are transformed in maturity, in life-skills, in leadership and in the many traits discussed in "Ten Kingdom Things Business Can Do." Through work, we create value for others, enabling us to fulfill the second-greatest commandment, to "love our neighbor," and the greatest commandment, to "love the Lord our God" (Matt. 22:36-40).

In the next chapter we'll see how work gets redefined as worship, and what a powerful thing it is to work as for the Lord.

CHAPTER 6

working as for the lord

One of the fundamental principles of Marketplace Christianity is working as for the Lord, as it says in Colossians 3:23:

Whatever you do, work at it with all your heart, as working for the Lord, not for men. Colossians 3:23 (NIV)

This revelation is so powerful that if even one person at the lowest level job gets it, it can change an entire company.

When I was leading my business a few years ago, many of the believers in the company asked me to hold a meeting and talk from a Christian perspective about my vision for the company. I did that, sharing quite a bit with them, and then one of the brothers shared his revelation of working as for the Lord. The atmosphere suddenly became electric. Something clicked for me and many others in the room who had longed to express our love for God.

Those same people who had hung their heads without spiritual purpose, suddenly had purpose. We had been given the key.

We began working as for the Lord, and within a short amount of time, many people who occupied the lowest rung on the company hierarchy became heroes of the company because they embraced this concept. Their exploits became well known throughout the whole workplace. Some of them rocketed up the company ladder, while others stayed in their positions and became the most honored and respected individuals amongst their bosses and peers.

> **Wherever a believer works as for the Lord, a revival happens in his or her heart, and then it spreads to those around him**

Without doing anything conspicuous to gain notice, these heroes raised the bar for all the believers in the company. Lukewarm Christians began recovering their passion; many began emulating the heroes by working as for the Lord. Unbelievers became curious; many were touched and perplexed as for the first time they were confronted with an authentic, non-programmed Christianity for which they had no argument or debate. This was a religion of the heart, not a religion of the head. The extraordinary love motive of these men and women became apparent to all. Much of the water-cooler conversation turned to God, religion and the Bible. Many unbelievers received Jesus. The atmosphere was often filled with the joy of the Lord and the presence of God.

Wherever a believer works as for the Lord, a revival happens in his or her heart, and then it spreads to those around him. Why is this principle so powerful? Firstly, because it invites the presence of God into a situation and a place. When He comes, things change. As the Bible says,

> ³ *For by their own sword they did not possess the land,*
> *And their own arm did not save them,*
> *But Your right hand and Your arm and <u>the light of Your</u>*
> <u>*presence,*</u>
> *For You favored them. Ps. 44:3 (NASB)*

Secondly, working as for the Lord is the opposite of how the world operates. The world works out of selfishness, pride and greed, rarely love. Working

working as for the Lord is the opposite of how the world operates

from a heart of love makes us like a light set on a hill:

> ¹⁴ *"You are the light of the world. A city set on a hill cannot be hidden; ¹⁵ nor does anyone light a lamp and put it under a basket, but on the lampstand, and it gives light to all who are in the house. ¹⁶ Let your light shine before men in such a way that they may see your good works, and glorify your Father who is in heaven." Matt. 5:14-16 (NASB)*

This principle of "working as for the Lord" is so important to the Christian faith, it is set forth twice – the dual witness of scripture – in Colossians 3:22-24 and Ephesians 6:5-8:

> ²² *Slaves, obey your earthly masters in everything; and do it, not only when their eye is on you and to win their favor, but with sincerity of heart and reverence for the Lord. ²³ Whatever you do,*

work at it with all your heart, as working for the Lord, not for men,
²⁴since you know that you will receive an inheritance from the
Lord as a reward. It is the Lord Christ you are serving. Col. 3:22-
24 (NIV)

⁵Slaves, obey your earthly masters with respect and fear, and with
sincerity of heart, just as you would obey Christ. ⁶Obey them not
only to win their favor when their eye is on you, but like slaves of
Christ, doing the will of God from your heart. ⁷Serve
wholeheartedly, as if you were serving the Lord, not men, ⁸because
you know that the Lord will reward everyone for whatever good he
does, whether he is slave or free. Eph. 6:5-8 (NIV)

Working as for the Lord can be broken into five key components.

1. Changing Bosses

Who's your boss? A drill sergeant? A spouse? Your parents? A teacher? The supervisor at your company? Your regional manager? Here's the first good news: When you work as for the Lord, that person is no longer your boss. In your heart, you will now work for the Lord. Paul wrote, "it *[really]* is the Lord we are serving" (Col. 3:24).

Though your tasks come from human beings, you don't do it for them, but for God and God alone

Though your tasks come from human beings, you don't do it for them, but for God and God alone ("serving the Lord, *not men*" – Eph. 6:7). If your earthly boss is pleased, that's a plus, but it's not what you seek. You'll have a godly ambivalence about human opinion, as Brother Lawrence stated in the book *The Practice of the Presence of God*: "The most excellent method I have found of going to God is that of doing common business without any view to pleasing men, as far as I am capable, doing it purely for the love of God."

Working for the Lord creates interesting paradoxes. Though men dictate our tasks, we look to God alone for our feedback. When humans give us feedback, we listen attentively, humbly and thankfully, seeking any way we might improve our service. But we do not seek their approval. Jesus said, "I do not accept praise from men" (John 5:41). Neither must we.

I recall the first time I spoke publicly in church. I was terrified, because I knew how much I wanted the praise of my pastor and friends — and I knew this was wrong. I prayed God would help me close my ears to my brothers and sisters. Afterward, people came to encourage me, so I greeted them but tried to close my ears to what they were saying. As soon as I was done, I ran home and asked God how He thought I did.

Those who anchor their lives to the praise of man will be tossed around like a dry leaf, and they will never come into their true purpose

There was a day when my company was the toast of our city. Every word spoken or written gushed with praise and adulation. When we hit hard times a few years later, we became an object of scorn. I learned that the praise of men is as fickle as the wind. Those who anchor their lives to it will be tossed around like a dry leaf, and they will never come into their true purpose. It is impossible to serve both God and men. The praise of man and the scorn of man are two sides of the same coin. The praise of men is an ever-shifting goal, but the Lord is constant, and unchanging. He knows our hearts, and He is so easy to please. He makes a much better Master! Those who accept praise from men are doomed to slavishly serve them. As Jesus said, "How can you *believe*, when you accept praise from men?" (John 5:44).

Neither do we seek our reward with men, but rather a heavenly reward (Matt. 6:19-20). The same is true of promotion.

No Ambition, No Territorialism, No Politics

By changing bosses, we unseat one of the most dominant spiritual forces at work in the world: the political spirit. This is a spirit of self-promotion. The dictionary defines it as, "Intrigue or maneuvering within a political unit or a group in order to gain control or power." The political spirit crucified Jesus, and it will persecute wholehearted believers in the workplace, because we are a threat to that spirit.

> By changing bosses, we unseat one of the most dominant spiritual forces at work in the world: the political spirit

The scriptures are filled with warnings to stand against the political spirit. It is called "selfish ambition." In Gal. 5:20 it is listed as one of the deeds of the flesh, alongside immorality, impurity, idolatry and witchcraft. We are told it is a root of much evil:

[16]*For where jealousy and selfish ambition exist, there is disorder and every evil thing. James 3:14 (NASB)*

We are told to keep selfish ambition from our hearts:

[3]Let nothing be done through selfish ambition or conceit, but in lowliness of mind let each esteem others better than himself. Phil. 2:3 (NKJV)

All true promotion comes from God, and we should choose to take the last seat until the Master himself comes to promote us (Luke 14:7-11). King David followed this principle, never promoting himself but waiting for God to unequivocally promote him. Though it took longer, he knew it was the Lord's work, not his. Later, his son Absalom tried to promote himself by gathering an entourage and asserting his claim to the throne. Jesus' parable in Luke 14 tells us that those who promote themselves will be demoted by God. In the end, Absalom was killed violently and the country was torn apart.

> **By trusting God to promote us and to honor us in the sight of others if it is His will, we break from the spirit of self-promotion**

The spirit of the world is self-promotion. Everyone everywhere is trying to climb over their peers to get ahead. By trusting God to promote us and to honor us in the sight of others if it is His will, we break from the spirit of self-promotion and it is a stunning, perplexing testimony to those around us.

My older brother's first job was as a test technician working on a PC-board assembly line. As a board came off the line, he plugged it into a testing unit to see if it was functional. It was a menial and boring job. The more desirable job was re-work engineering –

diagnosing and repairing boards that failed. The company always hired re-work engineers from amongst the test technicians, which caused the technicians to fight for dominance, claiming credit for good work and blaming others for bad work, constantly bad-mouthing each other. My brother wanted a re-work job badly and did what everyone else did, tearing others down and promoting himself. But after more than a year he kept getting passed by, even though he was one of the best workers. Finally he decided to stop tearing down others and forget about the promotion. He started raving about the work of others, doing his best to help them succeed and look good. To his surprise, he was the next re-work engineer hired.

2. Treating Our Tasks as from God

Once we change bosses, we are to obey our earthly bosses *"just as we would obey Christ"* (Eph 6:5). Even though our tasks are dictated by others, we are to treat them as if they come directly from the throne of God. Then we become "like *slaves of Christ*, doing the will of God from our heart" (Eph. 6:6). By viewing our tasks this way, several things happen.

> **Even though our tasks are dictated by others, we are to treat them as if they come directly from the throne of God**

1. We become wholehearted. Our two scriptures tell us to "serve wholeheartedly" (Eph. 6:7), working "with all our heart" (Col. 3:23). Wholehearted means our heart is not divided between the job at hand and our desire to do some other ministry work. Rather, the job at hand *is* our ministry work. Because it is really the Lord

we are serving in our tasks, then it is impossible for us to be less than completely wholehearted. In sharp contrast to this biblical mandate, modern Christians are generally the worst workers on the planet, precisely because they are not *wholehearted*, but *divided-hearted*. Their hearts are divided between work and ministry. They give little at work because their hearts are somewhere else. Early in my career, I went to work as late as I could, I left as early as I could, and gave as little as I could, but got as much money as I could.

> Because it is really the Lord we are serving in our tasks, then it is impossible for us to be other than completely wholehearted

2. We become extraordinarily committed and dedicated, "obeying in *everything*" (Col 3:22), because we know we're serving the Lord. We serve without reservation or hesitation because "we are doing the express will of God" (Eph 6:6). Some ask me, "What if we are told to do something immoral?" Obviously, immoral tasks are not from God. Most immoral acts are also illegal or unethical. We should discourage our bosses from immorality, and if they persist, we must oppose it and expose it, not from a place of high-handed moral superiority, but humility and the fear of God.

Others ask me how to keep from being taken advantage of and run into the ground by an earthly boss. My first answer is that this truly is a radical lifestyle. Many situations that seem unjust must be endured and given to God to worry about. On the other hand, we must also defend family and other commitments God gives us. Sometimes we must refuse a boss's demand that conflicts with something else of value in our lives. But before we refuse, we should diligently seek the Lord for His guidance in choosing between commitments. Years ago I worked for a very hard man. Every day I would ask the Lord if I could leave and find another job. I always felt the Lord say, "No, not yet." Then one day the man exploded and threatened me in a fit of rage. After that I knew it was time to move on, and I did.

3. We will serve in reverence and the fear of the Lord. Our two scriptures instruct us to work in "reverence for the Lord" (Col. 3:22) and "with respect and fear" (Eph. 6:5).

This means having a deep-seated weightiness about our tasks because we know we are fulfilling a holy commission. For example, if an angel appeared to me and spoke to me about writing a new kind of computer code, it would produce in me fear of the Lord regarding my task. This is how seriously He takes your work and mine: *He* is commissioning it, *He* is entrusting us with it and *He* will examine it. The Lord has given us a holy commission, which we are privileged and honored to participate in – we have a responsibility to discharge our duty well. That sense of responsibility is the "fear of the Lord." It means recognizing the responsibility we bear, and the incredible opportunity we have to co-labor with Him.

4. We will readily embrace even menial, distasteful and undesirable tasks, knowing they are from God. By doing jobs no

one else wants, we can secretly rejoice, because it is an opportunity to serve God for love's sake alone. "But the brother of humble circumstances is to glory in his high position" (James 1:9).

I was leading a meeting at my business one morning, and I asked for a volunteer to carry the emergency pager. Nobody wanted the job because it meant responding to computer emergencies, usually in the middle of the night. As I scanned the room, everyone stared intently at the floor. Then one of my heroes raised his hand and said, "I'll do it." He was smiling. Everyone else in the room looked at him, mouths agape. Some understood, but plenty did not, that he was serving God in love.

> **By doing jobs no one else wants, we can secretly rejoice, because it is an opportunity to serve God for love's sake alone**

At another time, late one Friday night after nearly everyone had gone home, our computer systems crashed in such a way that nearly all our customers were immediately affected. Our customer care call center was quickly overrun with calls. Phones started ringing throughout the building. One of our other heroes was just getting ready to leave, but instead he stayed nearly all night, then came in all weekend to field calls from angry customers. I learned about what he'd done on Monday at the "executive water cooler" from several of the executives who couldn't contain their astonishment. This man was a fairly senior person in the company, the executive assistant of one the senior executives, and it was well known he was a dedicated family man.

Because our boss is the Lord and He sees everything, we will do everything well, even when no one is looking. We'll pour our best work into even the small, unseen and hidden things, for our "Father, who sees what is done in secret, will reward" us (Matt. 6:4).

After hearing one of my teaching tapes on this topic, one young man resigned his ministry position and took a job in a local restaurant as a server (I am not recommending this!). He began working as for the Lord. Within *six weeks*, he was chosen as server of the *year*. He commented privately to one of my friends, "I would die for Jesus as a server."

When we treat our tasks as coming from the Lord, we become the best workers the planet has ever seen. We throw ourselves at our work without reservation or hesitation, because it is His will we're doing. One time our company physically relocated our data center – a hugely complicated task fraught with risk. After it had been completed successfully, I heard (again, at the executive water-cooler) that

We'll pour our best work into even the small, unseen and hidden things

one of my heroes, *without being asked*, had brought his sleeping bag into the data center and slept there several nights in case something went wrong. The executives were astonished and perplexed at what motivated this man.

Another company hero was famous for going the extra mile for customers. He would stay up all night if necessary to work with a customer. He astonished co-workers and bosses because there was simply no limit to what he would do for a customer. More astonishingly, he carried out every task with a smile, a belly-laugh and a good word, even when he was exhausted and under stress.

Another hero was known as the king of customer service. He was extremely meticulous in solving customer problems and wouldn't stop until the problem was completely resolved in the customer's eyes. To him, quality was everything because it was going to have God's name on it, it had to be good. Many customers became so enamored of him they refused to be handled by anyone else. We ended up building our entire customer service department around this employee's practices.

When we work as for the Lord, others may be threatened, or perceive our work ethic as "brown-nosing." But at the same time it will perplex them, because it is clear we are not playing the political game and because there is an aroma of contentedness about us.

> **What "counts" to God is not the task but the motivation of our hearts**

3. Changing Motives

This is perhaps the most important principle in this book. Simply put, love for God must be our single motive, the engine driving all our actions within the marketplace. When this is true, it does not matter the level of worker we are — CEO or janitor — we can completely fulfill our calling and store up heavenly rewards because what "counts" to God is not the task but the motivation of our hearts.

Some people despair because they are "stuck" in a job that appears to have no Kingdom purpose. They are like the slaves of 2,000 years ago, spending their lives chained in the bottom of ship, pulling oars like in a scene out of *Ben Hur*. What chance did those slaves have to engage in ministry activities? None, it would seem. Undoubtedly, some thought they could never store up heavenly rewards, never fully realize their calling or purpose in the marketplace.

Many Marketplace Christians today feel that way. I mentioned my wife's example. I well remember Lauren breaking down in tears, utterly distraught after the birth of our third child because she was no longer able to pass out tracts and witness to students at the nearby college campus. She had lost control over her time because of her obligation to our kids. She loved God so much, how could she do his work now?

A slave could not control his own destiny or do traditionally-defined "kingdom works," yet a slave could earn a heavenly reward

But the Bible speaks to each of us as "bondslaves of Christ" when it says,

> [22] *Slaves, obey your earthly masters in everything;* [24] *since you know that you will receive an inheritance from the Lord as a reward. Col. 3:22,24 (NIV)*

This is an earth-shattering truth! A slave could not control his own destiny or do traditionally-defined "kingdom works," *yet a slave could earn a heavenly reward*, the same as any of the apostles. Paul confirmed this when he wrote,

⁶The only thing that counts is faith expressing itself through love. Gal. 5:6 (NIV)

Kingdom service *at any level* counts when our work is motivated by love. We might be scrubbing toilets or making million-dollar decisions, but in God's sight, all that matters is the motivation of our hearts. The lowest paid toilet-scrubber in Donald Trump's empire has the same opportunity to lay up heavenly rewards and fulfill his purpose as Trump himself, even if the toilet-scrubber never advances up the job ladder.

Motivation is everything to God. Jesus rebuked the Ephesian church, the single greatest revival center of its day and the hub of Holy Spirit activity in Asia Minor, saying:

The lesson of Ephesus is that the Kingdom of God is not about works but about love

²I know your deeds, your hard work and your perseverance. ... ⁴Yet I hold this against you: You have forsaken your first love. ⁵Remember the height from which you have fallen! Repent and do the things you did at first. If you do not repent, I will come to you and remove your lampstand from its place. Rev. 2:2, 4-5 (NIV)

The lesson of Ephesus is that the Kingdom of God is not about works but about love. In the end, whether you're a governor or a wage-earner, a leader or a follower, a CFO or a secretarial assistant, your spiritual impact does not come from your work but from your motivation. Paul wrote,

¹If I speak with the tongues of men and of angels, but do not have love, I have become a noisy gong or a clanging cymbal. ²If I have the gift of prophecy, and know all mysteries and all knowledge; and if I have all faith, so as to remove mountains, but do not have love, I am nothing. ³And if I give all my possessions to feed the poor, and if I surrender my body to be burned, but do not have love, it profits me nothing. 1 Cor. 13:1-3 (NASB)

He makes it abundantly clear that if love is not our motive, even the grandest of Kingdom works are fuel for the fire.

As we work as for the Lord with hearts motivated by love, work becomes an act of worship. Worship can be more than a song. It can be *anything we do to "love Him back."* It is doing a job joyfully, giving, being a good mother, or taking care of your elderly parents. God is able to receive love in any form. We worship Him by doing whatever our job demands, as the Bible says,

Worship can be more than a song. It can be anything we do to "love Him back."

Whatever your hand finds to do, do it with all your might Eccl 9:10 (NASB).

Change your motivation and *any work you do* will become Kingdom work and will establish the Kingdom of God.

I recall a few years back, one of my young sons was watching his mother get ready for her day. He observed attentively as she searched for a particular piece of jewelry in the pile in her drawer. She couldn't find what she needed – everything was tangled and nothing matched. She was making mild exclamations of frustration as she rummaged in vain. My son was taking all this in, and I could see the wheels turning in his mind. Soon he disappeared. A while later, he ran back to his mother and held out his creation, saying, "Mom, I made something for you." It was an elaborate jewelry tree – several bowls for earrings, arms of various lengths for necklaces and bracelets, with a base and struts – all carefully manufactured from cardboard and duct tape. It was undoubtedly the most homely jewelry tree ever made. But to her it didn't matter what it looked like – it is her prized possession and to this day it stands as a symbol of his love.

What gift can we possibly give to the God who has everything? The same gift my son gave to his mother. She didn't need his jewelry tree – she could have bought a better one. But his love made the gift a treasure. If he had another motive – for instance, if he had tried to bargain with it for something in return – it would have been worthless to her.

> **God does not look for our gifts, but for the love that makes our gifts acceptable**

This is a human illustration of a key truth of the Kingdom. God does not look for our gifts, but for the love that makes our gifts acceptable. If love is in our heart, *anything* we offer to God is acceptable. Whether or not we want to accept it, all our best "Kingdom works" are made of "cardboard and duct tape" to God. But that does not diminish them in the eyes of the Father. Many of us can feel like our meager offering is too worthless to give. But we must be like the widow with her mites: *what she had, she gave.* Others of us look at what we have been given, and we see only cardboard and duct tape. But like my son, we simply need to *use the tools we have been given*:

> [12] *For if the willingness is there, the gift is acceptable according to what one has, not according to what he does not have. 2 Cor. 8:12 (NIV)*

According to this definition of worship, every human being can worship God every day, all day long. Our entire life, all of our activities, regardless of our station, can be a continuum of love and worship to God. How much of our lives we have wasted by making it loveless! We have robbed God of worship, and robbed our hearts of purpose and joy.

> **Our entire life, all of our activities can be a continuum of love and worship to God**

Earlier, we discussed how we been robbed of purpose for the 99 percent of our lives that exist outside of ministry arenas. But this was not to be so, in New Testament Christianity: we are to bring God into our activities (1 Cor. 7:24), and do everything for the love of God (Col 3:23). Suddenly, that 99 percent of life outside of ministry activities becomes meaningful.

4. Being Unashamed

Many believers mistakenly believe that their primary obligation in the workplace is to preach. For some this might be true, but for most it is not. Many misconstrue the Great Commission of Matt 28 and Mark 16 as their personal mandate. But this mandate was directed at the apostles and the church at large; furthermore, in

Mark 16, the mandate was not to be with words alone, but with the power of God.

Most believers are eager to witness for their faith, but feel completely helpless because they don't know what to say. But the Lord does not require us to be know-it-all Bible-bangers. Rather, our Gospel is primarily of love and power. When we demonstrate love by working for the Lord, we demonstrate the power of God in the human heart. Paul said,

> **When we demonstrate love by working for the Lord, we demonstrate the power of God in the human heart**

My message and my preaching were not in persuasive words of wisdom, but in demonstration of the Spirit and of power, so that your faith would not rest on the wisdom of men, but on the power of God (1 Cor. 2:5).

Titus 2:9 tells us:

[9]Teach slaves to be subject to their masters in everything, to try to please them, not to talk back to them, [10]and not to steal from them, but to show that they can be fully trusted, so that in every way they will make the teaching about God our Savior attractive. (NIV)

Our actions generate curiosity, perplexity and respect in unbelievers, and we must be ready to share our faith when asked:

[15]Always be prepared to give an answer to everyone who asks you to give the reason for the hope that you have. But do this with gentleness and respect." 1 Peter 3:13 (NIV)

We are not required to be sophisticated apologists for the faith like Paul or Apollos. Our Gospel is designed for simple, uneducated slaves. Many people get stuck sharing the faith, because they feel they cannot win a debate. However, *our most effective sharing is not articulated theses, but a living testimony.*

I used to preach extensively on college campuses, and I learned a critical truth about sharing the Gospel. When I *preached*, it became a *debate*. When I shared my *personal testimony*, critics fell silent.

> **Our personal testimony, shared respectfully, and backed by a life that demonstrates true love, will almost always be well-received**

How can you argue against someone's personal story? Revelation 12:11 says the saints overcame by the *word of their testimony*. When people ask us about our faith, we don't have to offer well-packaged words. We simply need to share part of our personal journey.

Jesus exhorts us to be completely unashamed in our faith:

[26] *"For whoever is ashamed of Me and My words, the Son of Man will be ashamed of him when He comes in His glory, and the glory of the Father and of the holy angels." Luke 9:26 (NASB)*

We have nothing to be ashamed of! God has touched our hearts! Sometimes we are ashamed because we know our words will sound foolish. But our personal testimony, shared respectfully, and backed by a life that demonstrates true love, will almost always be well-received.

How to Share Your Faith

Here is a simple tip for sharing your faith. Whenever I felt God wanting me to reach someone for him, I would invite them out to lunch. I would ask them to tell their story, while I would listen enthusiastically. I would find out their victories, their failures, their pains, their hopes and dreams, and what makes them "tick." It never failed, that they would after a time (sometimes after the second or third lunch) that my story would come up. I would share how God touched my heart and everything changed inside – that now I love God and want to please him, even though I am not very good at it. Most people are extremely intrigued about faith and ask lots of questions if they feel they can ask them without being offensive. And because of the friendship being built, they became comfortable asking personal questions.

> Once this kind of friendship is established, it is easy and natural to share with them or pray with them

I never felt the need to fully answer all their questions. Even if you know the answers, they can sometimes be a distraction from the real issues. As Paul said, "I determined to know nothing among you except Jesus Christ, and him crucified" (1 Cor. 2:2). I would often shake my head and reply, "I don't really have a good answer for that; all I know is he really loves me, and I love him back, and everything is different inside."

Once this kind of friendship is established, it is easy and natural to share with them or pray with them. When they are telling you about a fight with their spouse, or a tough family situation, or financial difficulties, you tell them God really answers prayer and offer to pray with them. Go to an empty office or a car and pray.

Christian Jihad?

After I taught at a seminar one day, the CFO of a large company expressed his indignation over the "homosexual agenda" being advanced at his workplace. He felt it was time to take a stand and publicly fight the homosexuals, though he thought it would cost him his job. He was animated and angry.

> **Jesus came meekly as a lamb, and clearly instructed us to do the same**

This poor man had completely missed his mission on earth. I told him "he did not know the spirit he was of" (Luke 9:54-55). We are not here to stop all sinners from sinning, or to destroy those who resist God. Jesus is not trying to judge sinners (John 3:17; 12:47-48) – he is trying to woo them to himself through love. They are already judged (John 3:18), and there is a terrible day when their judgment is declared final, but until then, he is granting them a wonderful window of mercy. Our prayer should not be for them to be judged – which is already assured – but it should be that God would forgive them and grant them mercy.

Jesus came meekly as a lamb, and clearly instructed us to do the same. There will be a day when he returns as the judge of the earth, but that is in the next age, not this one. Our job not to judge and condemn, but to love and have compassion:

43 "You have heard that it was said, 'You shall love your neighbor and hate your enemy.' *44 "But I say to you, love your enemies and pray for those who persecute you,* *45 so that you may be sons of your Father who is in heaven; for He causes His sun to rise on the evil and the good, and sends rain on the righteous and the unrighteous.* *46 "For if you love those who love you, what reward do you have? Do not even the tax collectors do the same?* *47 "If you greet only your brothers, what more are you doing than others? Do not even the Gentiles do the same?* *48 "Therefore you are to be perfect, as your heavenly Father is perfect. Matthew 5:43-48 (NASB)*

Overcoming Intimidation

In some workplaces, the spirit of intimidation can be strong and profound. As I was sharing these principles with people who worked in large, powerful Wall Street firms, I could see wide-eyed fear. "My co-workers will devour me alive!" they seemed to say.

First, in hostile situations, we should pray and ask God for help. We must realize that this irrational fear is a demonic power. We should ask God to lead us to other believers so we can gather with them to pray. I strongly encourage believers in these environments to ask God to lead them to other believers in their organization and start a private prayer meeting, focusing on asking for the Kingdom of God to come in the organization. Resolve to stay steadfast in prayer no matter what happens, for as long as it takes. Within a few months, everything will begin to change. Over and over I have seen agitators and persecutors suddenly removed, key policies changed, and the atmosphere completely shifted.

Believers must realize they have authority to establish God's kingdom in the earth – including their workplaces. If there are only two believers in a huge corporation, those two believers have more spiritual authority than the thousands of others combined. "If *my* people who are called by *my* name humble themselves and pray and seek My face and turn from their wicked ways, then I will hear from heaven, will forgive their sin and will heal their land [workplaces]" (2 Chron. 7:14).

This is part of our mandate as individual believers – we have both the privilege and the responsibility of establishing God's reign on the planet. Our weapons are love, humility, faith and prayer, and they are powerful for the destruction of evil and the establishment of righteousness in the earth (2 Cor. 10:4).

Believers must realize they have authority to establish God's kingdom in the earth – including their workplaces.

Second, we must get over our fear of backlash. We need to trust God to provide for His own. The authority of our persecutors is limited. As Esther went before the King to plead for the Jews, she took her life in her hands. She said, "If I die, I die." In some sense, we must do the same.

Finally, we must be ready to be persecuted. After sharing the principles of "working as for the Lord" to a group of interns, one young man retorted to me, "it doesn't work!" He explained angrily to me how he gave his whole heart at work, as for the Lord, and as a result was mocked and mistreated.

I asked him, "So you did nothing wrong?"

"That's right," he nodded vigorously.

"You were just 'doing righteousness' and loving Jesus?"

"That's right," he agreed again, more hurt than ever.

"And you were persecuted?"

> **If we are persecuted because we are working as for the Lord, then our reward is great**

"Yes," he replied, freshly feeling the pain of how terribly wronged he was.

"So it would be safe to say, for righteousness' sake you were persecuted?"

Suddenly he was taken aback as he realized where I was going. I laughed, "Rejoice!!! *Great* is your reward in heaven!" If we are persecuted because we are working as for the Lord, then our reward is great! Jesus said,

[11]Blessed are you when people insult you, persecute you and falsely say all kinds of evil against you because of me. [12]Rejoice and be glad, because great is your reward in heaven. Matt. 5:11-12 (NIV)

It's a high honor to be counted worthy of suffering for righteousness' sake, alongside Jesus!

5. Constant Communion

The fifth element of working as for the Lord is the most blessed: constant communion with God. In Matthew 7:21, Jesus said He will denounce some who worked miracles for Him, saying, "I never *knew* you." Since God knows all things, Jesus is not speaking of factual knowledge – He is speaking of intimate knowledge. The Bible equates knowledge and intimacy: "Adam *knew* Eve and she conceived" (Genesis 4:1). We practice and pursue intimacy with God by engaging in constant communion with Him. This is the greatest endeavor upon which the human heart can embark. What an unbelievable privilege He invites us into — communion with the God of the universe! Who are *we*? Flesh and blood, wicked and selfish and many other things — and yet the Maker of all creation extends His very heart to us.

> **Intimacy with God is the greatest endeavor upon which the human heart can embark**

Most of us are task-oriented, looking to the result as the prize, while the process of getting there is something we chafe under and endure. But God is journey-oriented. He gives us tasks not only for the result, but so we can co-labor in them and grow. I recently bought my two boys plastic models of ships. I didn't buy them because I wanted them to have plastic ships. I didn't buy them so they could build ships for me because I wanted ships. I bought them so that we could do something together. So it is with God.

To rush past the journey toward the goal is to miss the best part! If we raised children only to turn them into adults, we'd miss the whole point of sharing lives together, growing together, loving together. As one of my friends says, "The journey is the reward."

Work and communion ought not to be separate activities. David discovered intimacy with God while working as a shepherd. All of life is to be a continuum of worship and communion.

I used to be baffled by 1 Thes. 5:17 where we are told to "pray continually." I thought prayer meant a *prayer meeting*. But I learned that we can pray continually by engaging in a running conversation with God. When I worked as an engineer, I could not engage in continual conversation because my job required the full use of my thoughts. But throughout the day during "thought breaks" I would turn my thoughts to God and converse with Him.

> **David discovered intimacy with God while working as a shepherd. All of life is to be a continuum of worship and communion**

Colossians 3:2 instructs us to "set our minds on things above." This is as easy as extending our thoughts toward God, inviting Him into our everyday stream of inner conversation. The Bible promises,

[8]*Draw near to God and He will draw near to you. James 4:8 (NASB)*

It is that simple to walk in the presence of God. If He is with us, we will have peace and joy; and we can endure anything. The Westminster Catechism of 1647 states profoundly: "Man's chief end is to glorify God, and to *enjoy him for ever.*" Psalm 37:4 commands us to "delight ourselves in the Lord!" In Psalm 40:8, David says, "I *delight* to do your will." It is our purpose to enjoy God, every day, all day long!

Brother Lawrence was a seventeenth-century French monk who spent his entire life practicing the presence of God in his mundane chores. Though he never wrote a book, he was a marvel in his time. People traveled from all over the world to learn from him. For Lawrence, life was entirely about communing with God:

"My set times of prayer are not different from other times of the day. Although I do pray (because it is the direction of my superior) I do not need such retirement nor do I ask for it because my greatest business does not divert me from God. ... I have found that we can establish ourselves in a sense of the presence of God by continually talking with Him. It is simply a shameful thing to quit conversing with Him to think of trifles and foolish things. We should feed and nourish our souls with high notions of God which will yield great joy. ... You need to accustom yourself to continual conversation with Him – a conversation which is free and simple. We need to recognize that God is always intimately present with us and address Him every moment." – Brother Lawrence, The Practice of the Presence of God.

Communion with God brings great joy, as the Bible says,

In your presence is fullness of joy. Psalm 16:11 (NASB)

In my business, there was often a supernatural joy accompanying the presence of God. Many of my heroes walked in a continuous joy. They served with a smile in their hearts toward God. Their primary mission was to enjoy God every day. That joy, flowing from constant communion with God, became a powerful testimony to others.

A Revival Waiting to Happen

The good news about working as for the Lord is that it empowers every Marketplace Christian in every task to revolutionize his or her workplace. The strategy of heaven has never been to take important, rich, educated, brilliant and gifted people and through them convince the world God has a better idea. God took the poor, the uneducated, the inarticulate and the slaves. He put in them a hope and a love that surpassed anything ever seen, and within three centuries that primitive Christianity – the faith of slaves, the poor and the uneducated – conquered the greatest empire the earth has ever seen.

> The strategy of heaven has never been to take important, rich, educated, brilliant and gifted people and through them convince the world God has a better idea

Today, many Christians have forgotten who we are. We have polished our words, choreographed our meetings, built beautiful churches and dressed up the Gospel to make it appealing to a transient culture. But how many of us live lives consumed by love? We have teachings, tapes, books and exhortations galore, but little raw heart-power. We could very well be the generation of which it was prophesied: "the love of most will grow cold" (Matt. 24:12);

"wanting to have their ears tickled" (2 Tim. 4:3); "having a form of godliness but denying its power" (2 Tim. 3:5).

We must return to our heritage and let love be our motivation. We must express this love by working as for the Lord. Statisticians tell us that more than 10 million people in the United States call themselves born-again Christians. That is in excess of 5 percent of the workforce. *What if those people began working as for the Lord?* It would launch a revival unprecedented since the days of the early church.

Next we'll look at a practical plan for building anointed businesses — workplaces that encourage business success and Kingdom life.

CHAPTER 7

the anointed business model

By working as for the Lord, any believer can create pockets of revival in even the darkest, most ungodly work environments. But when the right environment is in place, revival can go much further, and the presence of God can pervade a workplace. The strategy for creating this environment lies in creating anointed businesses, one of the primary ways I believe Marketplace Christians will carry out their marketplace ministry in coming days.

I've written about how my business became an anointed business. Believe it or not, when I started the company, I had no such thing in mind. My colleagues and I unwittingly created an environment that was conducive to revival, and God (without my permission!) added the spark from heaven. To this day, I am often stopped in the city by people who once worked for the company. Believers and unbelievers alike tell me it was one of the formative experiences of their lives, and by far the best place they ever worked. Even customers tell me how much they enjoyed the company and the incredible people who worked there.

in the last days, businesses are to no longer be desolate wastelands of faith where people lose their fire for God

Looking back, I believe it was a miracle from God, but no more a miracle than a crop of wheat which grows when planted. I'm convinced that if Marketplace Christianity is to be the force God intends it to be, we must learn to build anointed businesses. God even prophesied about anointed businesses 2,500 years ago in the book of Isaiah. In the scripture below, when you see the word "land," think "business," as they both point to the means of wealth-production:

4 *It will no longer be said to you, "Forsaken,"*
Nor to your land will it any longer be said, "Desolate";
But you will be called, "My delight is in her,"
And your land, "Married";
For the LORD delights in you,
And to Him your land will be married.
Isa. 62:4 (NASB)

This tells us that in the last days, businesses are to no longer be desolate wastelands of faith where people lose their fire for God. Rather, our businesses are to be married – bound together in unity – to the Lord. He will inhabit our businesses. God is leading millions of believers to work as for the Lord, as we have discussed.

The next step is for many of those to start anointed businesses, or to convert their existing businesses into anointed businesses. That's how we create thriving centers of spiritual activity that powerfully impact lives, release new levels of finances into believers' hands and create a powerful Christian sub-economy, which God will use as the days unfold.

I am often asked why we should bother starting or running businesses — why not just work as for the Lord? The answer is that as an owner or leader we have the opportunity to create a spiritual environment and set the "DNA" for that workplace. As an entrepreneur, I encourage believers to start businesses. But be warned: owning and operating a business is very challenging and should only be undertaken by those who are truly gifted for it. Most businesses fail, "Christian" businesses even more so. However, for those who are able, we can create an environment that reflects our spiritual DNA and values.

> For those who are able, we can create an environment that reflects our spiritual DNA and values

I have spent time analyzing what happened at my company and why, and I have come up with a pattern for what I call the Anointed Business Model. When followed, I believe these five principles will produce revival in any organization.

The Un-Anointed Business Model

Before diving into the five principles of building an anointed business, let's clarify what an anointed business is *not*. Most of us know of "Christian" businesses which hire only Christians — not the most qualified people, but the most "spiritual" people. Usually they enforce rigorous standards of spirituality but eschew traditional business practices like using lawyers and writing business plans, because those things are perceived as carnal.

they consider faith a valid replacement for competence and wisdom

When hiring, they don't hire the most qualified person, but the most spiritual In general, *they consider faith a valid replacement for competence and wisdom.*

By necessity, they develop spiritual litmus tests (how often one goes to church, which church they attend, etc.) to grade people on spirituality. This always devolves into cronyism and a political spirit, because reward is subjective, not objective.

I have observed scores of businesses built on this model – and *not one has succeeded.* At the core, these businesses presume that the blessing of God is automatically theirs, if they maintain certain standards of spirituality. Therefore the focus is not on business excellence, but spirituality. Not only do these businesses fail, but they leave a negative perception of Christians as businesspeople, because they do not respect the marketplace and good business practices.

That is *not* what we mean when we talk about anointed businesses!

The Building Blocks of an Anointed Business

The Anointed Business Model requires three elements:

1) seed, which is passion for Jesus;

2) soil, which is the workplace environment we create; and

3) water and sunshine, which is teaching.

Each of these is present in the five principles below.

Principle #1: Hire Christians as 10 to 33 Percent of Your Workforce

In my business, I started out with 100 percent Christians. We prayed together regularly and had a wonderful working environment. But as the business grew, I couldn't find the talent I needed within the church world.

I knew that hiring unbelievers would change the dynamics within the business, and I was concerned about losing the **I hired unbelievers and the atmosphere did change – for the better** special spiritual atmosphere we had cultivated. But I liked the idea of mixing Christians and non-Christians, while still maintaining a spiritual but not overtly religious environment.

I hired unbelievers and the atmosphere did change – for the better. The believers still gathered and prayed and worshipped together, though not as part of the official workday. But something just as wonderful happened: the Christians began reaching out to the needs of others. Their inward focus took an outward turn. They ministered to others who very much needed ministry.

I was then able to compare how a business operated with 100 percent Christians, and how the same business operated with about 20 percent Christians, which is the "mix" we settled at. I discovered that a business entirely made up of Christians faces serious challenges. On a practical level, it's very difficult to find within Christian circles the highly specialized skill sets you need to build strong businesses – sales, engineering, marketing, management and so forth.

In my experience, Christians are simply "better" when mixed with unbelievers

Then, as you seek to hire only Christians, you necessarily create spiritual "litmus tests" for each potential employee. This is problematic because when someone calls himself or herself a Christian, it does not mean he or she is a good worker, or even that he or she is terribly spiritual.

To my surprise, I discovered something else: when there are too many Christians in an organization, they tend to become small-minded, focusing on themselves and their opinions, debate and controversy. Sometimes they even begin to attack and tear down each other. In my experience, Christians are simply "better" when mixed with unbelievers.

Christians are also much more professional with unbelievers in the mix. When we had predominantly Christian employees, I was frustrated by a distinct lack of professionalism. No matter what I would say, they thought the purpose of the organization was fellowship. Relationship took precedence over excellence. Sloppy performance was expected to be overlooked for the sake of "love." Chronic underachievement was acceptable as long as someone was a "good person." When I hired unbelievers, the level of professionalism in the organization grew. Unbelievers brought in the expectation that employees were to be professional, work hard and help the business succeed.

On the other hand, a business suffers if there are too few Christians, as there may not be enough spiritual "horsepower" to create a healthy spiritual environment. When their numbers are too small, Christians tend to hide in their bunkers. To get them out of their bunkers, they often need to have a safe environment with other believers.

> **When their numbers are too small, Christians tend to hide in their bunkers**

Believers are seed in the workplace. Jesus said of the Kingdom of God,

> *[33]He spoke another parable to them, "The kingdom of heaven is like leaven, which a woman took and hid in three pecks of flour until it was all leavened." Matt. 13:33 (NASB)*

As much as possible, Marketplace Christians should mix with non-Christians in the same work environment, allowing that seed of passion to grow, that yeast of the Kingdom to spread. But it's important to recognize that not all Christians carry the same amount of "passion seeds." Without judging anyone or building a theology around it, let me observe that Christians fall into three categories:

1) Can't-live-without-it Christians who are passionate, wholehearted and actively pursuing God; we'll call them the "passionate."

there must be a core of believers in the "passionate" category who live out the principle of working as for the Lord

2) Bottled-up Christians who sincerely believe and are faithful, but can't or won't release the passion inside of them; we'll call them the "sincere."

3) I-guess-so Christians of nominal faith who, if pressed, say they believe in God, and who try to be ethical, but for all practical purposes are indistinguishable from unbelievers; we'll call them the "nominal."

In terms of spiritual impact, I find it useful to group the nominal Christians with unbelievers, because their faith level is about the same. My experience taught me that the best mix for an anointed business is this:

10 to 33 percent passionate and sincere Christians;

67 to 90 percent unbelievers and nominal Christians.

Furthermore, it is critical that there be a core of believers in the passionate category who are truly living out the principle of working as for the Lord. It is their passion that will spark everyone else and initiate the chain-reaction that produces a spiritual oasis.

A side note about hiring: I am often asked how to hire Christians without violating laws and without creating spiritual litmus tests. I accomplished this in two ways. First, I often advertised for available positions in church bulletins. Second, I often hired by referral – I would ask my best heroes to bring in people they knew.

I am also asked if there are circumstances where it is acceptable to hire 100% Christians. The answer is: sometimes, especially if the business is really a *ministry* to others. For instance, I ran a small gourmet coffee cart inside a movie theater. The cart was staffed exclusively by believers who were taught to work as for the Lord and minister to customers as part of our school of ministry.

This principle has shown us the seed, which is the passion in the hearts of Christian people. The next three principles define the *soil* needed to create an anointed business.

> **In a people-oriented environment, people are valued for who they are, not just for what they do**

Principle #2: A People-Oriented Environment

In a *people-oriented environment,* people are valued for who they are, not just for what they do. A people-oriented environment promotes mentoring, learning, launching and growing. It respects the lives and choices of all, including unbelievers.

The opposite of this is the *driven environment,* which is characterized by striving and fear. Human striving and driven-ness are two of the greatest enemies of the presence of God.

One day early in my company's history, I got a call from an old friend. She was living in a distant city and was now a single mom and handicapped, unable to leave the house. She had heard I started a company and wanted to know if I had any job she could do from home, like answering emails. I told her no, because I had designed my call center so that the agents had to use computer systems at my location. But I wanted to help her, and I knew she was in a desperate situation. I spent the next week redeveloping my call center software so that it was internet-based. This was beneficial to the business because it gave me enormous flexibility in the call center, and I was able to hire her. She became one of my best heroes.

> **To Jesus all human beings are precious – He cannot inhabit a workplace where they are devalued or mistreated**

God cares about people as individuals. To treat them as work-units is to miss the reality of who they are in His sight. To Jesus all human beings are precious – He cannot inhabit a workplace where they are devalued or mistreated.

I know few business leaders who operate in the "fear of God" when it comes to their treatment of people at work, yet scripture clearly states that they will give account to God for their leadership:

[17]Obey your leaders and submit to them, for they keep watch over your souls as those who will give an account. Hebrews 13:17 (NASB)

Most business leaders will be shocked to discover that they will give account to God for how they treat people in and through their businesses. It is common for Christian leaders to engage in harsh and insensitive business practices, convinced that they are exonerated because "business is business" – as if their business dealings are somehow outside the realm of God's purview.

Isaiah 58 is a scathing rebuke to such practices. Isaiah is speaking to marketplace leaders who are pursuing spirituality with passion (in their case fasting), but whose spirituality has not extended to their business dealings:

Most business leaders will be shocked to discover that they will give account to God for how they treat people in and through their businesses

2   *They're busy, busy, busy at worship,*
    and love studying all about me.
    To all appearances they're a nation of right-living   people—
    law-abiding, God-honoring.
    They ask me, 'What's the right thing to do?'
    and love having me on their side.
3   *But they also complain,*
    'Why do we fast and you don't look our way?
    Why do we humble ourselves and you don't even notice?'
    "Well, here's why:
    "The bottom line on your 'fast days' is profit.
    You drive your employees much too hard.
6   *"This is the kind of fast day I'm after:*
    to break the chains of injustice,
    get rid of exploitation in the workplace,

free the oppressed,
  cancel debts.
Isaiah 58:2-3, 6 (TMNT)

They have confined their spirituality to purely religious expressions of faith – a "church spirituality" – and then are surprised when God does not respond to them. God is not impressed by a "church spirituality" that doesn't extend into our dealings in everyday life. To God it is hypocrisy. When directing, correcting or firing someone, we need to get God's heart for that situation. When dealing with employees, customers, vendors, and competitors we must seek their welfare, in love, kindness, and gentleness.

God is not impressed by a "church spirituality" that doesn't extend into our dealings in everyday life

Early on in my business experience, I had a hard time reconciling the apparent conflict of caring about people and pursuing excellence in business. I cared deeply about my employees – many were my friends. So I never fired or demoted anyone or put anyone on probation. As a result, I had severe quality problems. *By not judging underperformance, I was rewarding it.* By not judging underachievers, I was devaluing my best achievers. They became totally demoralized. I was forced to learn how to correct, re-deploy and even fire people without devaluing them as God-created human beings.

In every business, it is inevitable that we must fire people, correct them or lay them off. We cannot hesitate to do these things when necessary. But even in these difficult situations, we must do them in a spirit of love and respect, knowing we are dealing with human beings who are precious to our Lord.

Principle #3: A Secular, Merit-Based Environment

Reward and recognition in the anointed business must be impartial and merit-based, never spiritual. The alternative is an environment in which spiritual performance is somehow measured and factored in. This always degenerates into cronyism because spiritual performance can't be objectively measured. The rewards will end up going to those who have the best relationship with the boss. This cripples a work environment, puts wrong people in leadership and embitters employees. It encourages a political spirit and causes employees to engage in spiritual pretense as a means to reward and recognition.

> **Reward and recognition in the anointed business must be impartial and merit-based, never spiritual**

In a secular environment, there is no recognition or reward for spirituality. This is as it should be: God does not attempt to create obedience through bribery. Rather, our obedience is to be love-based. By not rewarding spirituality, we are encouraging people to truly work as for the Lord rather than receiving their reward in full here on earth. God forces no one to love Him, nor does He promise us earthly riches or reward in return for obedience – and neither should we.

Principle #4: Gospel-Safe

In describing the Anointed Business Model, I use the phrase, "secular but Gospel-safe." Gospel-safe means the organization is completely free of the spirit of intimidation that permeates most secular organizations. It means personal expressions of faith are fully allowed and encouraged, so long as they do not hinder the work, are not disrespectful to others and are not part of professional business.

As CEO, I instructed believers to be open and unashamed about their faith, but never to compel someone or be disrespectful. I also instructed managers to be open about their faith, but never to use their position of authority to force or even subtly encourage spirituality upon others. I was always open about my faith, both in private and in public, but I always shared it as my personal experience and testimony. I was careful to separate my spirituality from what I expected of others. I often shared my faith one-on-one with people and encouraged them to turn to God. But when I did so, I made it abundantly clear that I was not wearing my "boss" hat but my "friend" hat. I recall an instance where I was speaking to one of my employees about his performance. The conversation went something like this: "As your boss, it is clear that your work is suffering, and you seem distracted. You need to address these issues, or I will have no alternative but to make changes. But as your friend, I am telling you your personal life is a mess! How are you doing with God? Are you going to church?

> In describing the Anointed Business Model, I use the phrase, "secular but Gospel-safe."

There is an excellent program that could help…" And so on. I was careful to share as a "friend" only if I had cultivated a friendship relationship with the person and I felt such honest personal sharing would be invited. Otherwise, it would have been presumptuous, disrespectful and would have left people feeling violated. Many bold Christians have ignored this principle and have created offense, resentment and a resistance to the Gospel.

Principle #5: Teaching

Water and sunshine make seeds grow. Without them, good seed and good soil will lie dormant. In an anointed business, water and sunshine are biblical teaching and understanding. These help passionate seeds spring to life in the welcoming soil of a Gospel-safe environment. There are five key teachings which must be present to unlock the seeds:

Teaching #1: Living under the smile of God. In my opinion, it's impossible to be a good worker without living under the smile of God, which means knowing that God is pleased with you and loves you even when you make mistakes. If we don't understand this aspect of God's character, we can easily become like the man in the parable who hid his talent because he misunderstood his boss's nature (see Matt. 25). That man said,

"Master, I knew you to be a hard man, *reaping where you did not sow and gathering where you scattered no seed. And* I was afraid, *and went away and hid your talent in the ground." (Matt. 25:24-25).*

He *had a wrong view of God*, and so he failed as a worker. We, too, will cripple ourselves as Marketplace Christians if we view God as a hard, unloving taskmaster.

I read a recent survey that showed that only five percent of Christians feel loved by God most of the time, only two percent feel the Father is joyful, and just one percent feel the Father is pleased with them most of the time. This is tragic! How can you enjoy working for God if you believe He is angry or disappointed with you?

The fact is, God delights in us! We are *the garden of his delight* (Isa. 5:7, NASB) Even when we fall short or disobey, and God chooses to discipline us for our own good, this *never* overshadows His love for us. Joy is His primary emotion toward us. To live under His smile means embracing the reality that He delights in us as individuals and workers.

> **We, too, will cripple ourselves as Marketplace Christians if we view God as a hard, unloving taskmaster**

Teaching #2: Redefining worship. Marketplace Christians must understand that if love is in their heart, their work can be their expression of love back to God, and that by doing so, the Kingdom of God is established. When unbelievers see Christians going about their work with supernatural, authentic love springing from their hearts, they will be overcome with curiosity about where it comes from.

Teaching #3: Working as for the Lord. Christians must recover their vision for the workplace. They must stop thinking of themselves as drones and underlings and see themselves as lovers of God happy to serve Him in whatever capacity their talents and His blessings allow. Otherwise, the workplace will be a meaningless void, and Christians will simply go through the motions, never engaging their hearts in passion.

Teaching #4: Pursuing intimacy and practicing the presence of God. When we include the Lord in the simple daily activities of life, He dwells right where we are. His presence tenderizes other hearts and releases the activity of the Holy Spirit.

> **Marketplace Christians must understand that if love is in their heart, their work can be their expression of love back to God**

Teaching #5: Seeing the workplace as a place of ministry. Christians must see the workplace as their "field," their coworkers and customers as their "flock." By so doing, they step out of self-concern and become others-oriented.

Just as a farmer waters his seeds many times before they sprout, we must labor repeatedly to exercise and understand these principles. As we do, we will be empowered as never before to build anointed businesses which will transform our marketplaces.

CHAPTER EIGHT

priests in the marketplace

When ministers whisper behind closed doors that the marketplace is a dangerous place to send Christians, it's easy to get defensive. But the truth is *they are mostly right*. Too often, Marketplace Christians let their spirituality fall by the wayside. We have not tended well the gardens of our hearts. We have let our passion for God wane. By pursuing money and success, we have become mammon's servants. Our spiritual pursuit often dwindles to minimal, perfunctory acts — just enough to keep our heads above water. Our only spiritual intensity comes when we need to be rescued from some desperate life situation. In many cases we have disengaged from church, become cynical and developed an independent spirit. Fresh faith has been replaced with cold, hardened pragmatism. Most tragically, many of us have become prayerless. Prayerlessness is the final fruit of our unspirituality.

Many Marketplace Christians have created a new identity for themselves: the de-spiritualized Christian who is a successful leader and professional and has stature in the community, but who only dabbles around the edges in spiritual matters, leaving passionate, life-changing spirituality to others. Some claim a "proximity spirituality," meaning they consider themselves spiritual because they are involved in spiritual enterprises. They may be in authority over some spiritual work, but spiritual leadership without true spirituality is illegitimate and not from God. True spiritual authority is established in prayer. Consider Solomon, the greatest king in Israel's history. He had a private passageway built between his bedroom and the temple where he regularly sought God. The Queen of Sheba saw this and was thunderstruck (1 Kings 10; 2 Kings 16:18).

Historically and biblically, the majority of great *spiritual* leaders came from the *marketplace*. They were ranchers, soldiers, shepherds and workers – normal people, yet deeply spiritual. Yet few marketplace Christians today even try to walk in the footsteps of Nehemiah, David, Joseph or Abraham. In spiritual matters, Christian leaders in the marketplace have mostly taken a back seat. They may have a God-granted leadership gift, but they have abdicated spiritual leadership and authority to others. Biblical heroes refused to settle for spiritual mediocrity. Why have we abdicated spiritual greatness? Why have we said in our hearts, "I can never be a Nehemiah, a Joseph or an Abraham?" How has the enemy convinced us to set our aim so low? Every believer is one step away from spiritual greatness. Most of the heroes of the Bible were Marketplace Christians just like you and me. They had nothing more or less from God. They could have settled for spiritual mediocrity, but they chose to take that step toward greatness.

God has no secular, unspiritual roles in His Kingdom:

⁹But you are a chosen people, <u>a royal priesthood</u>, a holy nation, a people belonging to God, that you may declare the praises of him who called you out of darkness into his wonderful light. 1 Pet. 2:9 (NIV)

Every believer is to be first a priest, even a *king-priest*, meaning one with a kingly flavor. It is not enough to build careers or businesses and give money to the kingdom. It is not even enough to build anointed businesses. We have reduced spirituality to integrity at work, church attendance and giving in church offerings. While these are good, they fall far short of true spirituality. We must become priests of our own lives and our marketplace flock if Marketplace Christianity will have the transforming power God intends it to have.

> **We have reduced spirituality to integrity at work, church attendance and giving in church offerings**

Nehemiah is a scriptural type of king-priest. He was respected in the marketplace, a gifted "governor." He was anointed to lead and build. But he did not abdicate his calling as king-priest. He was a civic leader *and* a man of prayer. On one hand he initiated the reconstruction of the city of Jerusalem, organized the exiles and supervised the construction of the city. But he also called the nation to repentance, restored temple worship and became a spiritual patriarch to the exiles.

That's a good model for Marketplace Christians. Let's see how to reclaim our priesthood in the marketplace.

Prayerlessness

Spiritual greatness comes to those who simply pursue God earnestly; and pursuit of God begins and ends in prayer. Prayer is the single key to reclaiming our marketplace priesthood. But Marketplace Christians are not usually praying people. We give money, go to fellowship groups and prayer breakfasts – but we won't pray. Why? Some of us are discouraged by our weakness. Our past efforts at prayer have only left us disappointed. After years of

> Spiritual greatness comes to those who simply pursue God earnestly; and pursuit of God begins and ends in prayer

neglect, we find ourselves spiritually atrophied. As spiritual second-class citizens, it has become easier to just not try. Like Leah, we feel unlovely (Gen. 29:31). But weakness is not to be despised but embraced. God is not impressed by the strength of man, nor depressed by the weakness of man. He loves our earnest pursuit. Like my son and his jewelry tree, He does not look at the gift but the heart with which it is given. In our hearts we must only earnestly desire Him to please Him. We must simply be consistent in our weak pursuit in order to become spiritual men and women.

Many Marketplace Christians quit praying because they feel unclean and sinful. Adultery, pornography, pride, desire for glory, selfish ambition, fear and greed run rampant in the marketplace, and sometimes ensnare believers. David too was a weak and inwardly torn man. He knew he was one step away from sin. He committed a grievous murder in order to commit grievous adultery. Yet David did not allow his weakness to destroy his relationship with God. He did not hide from God, but ran to Him in repentance (Ps. 51). Astonishingly, God was pleased with him and called him a "man after God's own heart," because he understood the heart of God – that *God was for him, even in his weakness and sin.* If we find ourselves stuck in a place of sin, today is the day to turn and flee. Even in our addictions, God will

> **We must simply be consistent in our weak pursuit in order to become spiritual men and women**

forgive us seventy-seven times per day, every day. We must not give up, we must cry out to God every day asking His forgiveness and help, and we must humble ourselves and seek help from others.

I attended a Christian investor's conference with a friend and the theme was "making money to give to missions." During the opening presentation, the purpose of the conference was proclaimed and the participants were dubbed "men of impeccable character." But my friend had a dream that night that everyone at the conference was "tilted" – meaning their motives had become less than pure. God spoke in the dream that it was okay to be tilted, so long as we didn't lie and claim we weren't. *God could deal with the sin, but not with pretense.*

Among Marketplace Christians, as in the church generally, there is far too much pretense. Pretense is about looking good in the eyes of others – which is idolatry of other's opinions. In Acts 5, Ananias and Sapphira were struck dead for their sin – but they would have been without sin or shame at all had they simply said, "We're not ready to give everything, but we'll give a portion of our money." Instead, they lied about it.

God wants to take us out of that place of sin, spiritual sickness and pretense and into our full marketplace calling, which includes vibrant, passionate spirituality and an active, on-going prayer dialogue with God. We must recognize God as the Healer and Redeemer. He loves to forgive us, heal us and redeem our sins and spiritual sicknesses. It is part of His glory, and there is no shame in admitting these things to Him. There is only shame if we pretend we're without sin.

We must embrace a fresh view of prayer. Prayer is not a perfunctory "rescue me," or "make me more money." True prayer is never drudgery or fruitless exertion – what Mike Bickle calls "rock-pile" prayer. It's a loving interaction with our Father in heaven, whose love for us knows no bounds (John 3:16), who sings over us (Zeph. 3:17), who delights in us (Ps. 16:3, Isa. 5:7), who thinks about us night and day (Ps. 139:17-18), who longs to draw near to us (Matt. 23:37).

> God wants to take us out of that place of sin, spiritual sickness and pretense

Self-Reliance

Another block to prayer is the sickness of self-reliance. Marketplace Christians generally think of themselves as problem-solvers. They hate excuses, hate being needy. As such, prayer offends them. There is an inherent weakness and absurdity to it — and that by God's design. Prayer requires humility and recognition of weakness. It's the only way prayer works.

I used to excuse myself from praying by saying, "I am not an intercessor." I was happy to let the elderly ladies in the church gather in the basement to pray. Like me, most Marketplace Christians want someone else to do the praying. But prayer is every believer's calling. Humans were created, by design, to ask and receive, which is what prayer is.

> **Most Marketplace Christians want someone else to do the praying**

When we ask of God, we are inviting Him to invade earth. Though God owns the earth, He does not take His authority to traffic here unless we invite Him to. For example, say I own a house that I have leased to another family. If I hear their plumbing is clogged, I cannot just take my key and barge in. The family must invite me in, even though I own the property and have sovereign rights over it.

When we neglect prayer, we dis-invite God out of our circumstance and workplace. You may recall the tragic episode of August 2000 when the Soviet Submarine "Kursk" sank to the ocean bottom. Several nations stood by with rescue equipment, ready to try to save the trapped sailors. They only needed Russia's approval. They waited for over a week, until the sailors were all dead, because the Russian leaders were stuck in self-reliance.

God has answers waiting for us, like the ships waiting to help the Kursk. He wants us to ask, so that He can answer.

Lack of Internal Drive

Another enemy of prayer is lack of internal motivation. Our lives can get stuffed with distraction and dissipation, shouted down by a cacophony of internal and external noise, thoughts, worries and cares. Our culture screams at us through its venues of entertainment and on every street corner is another person sharing his or her opinion. Modern life is nothing if not disorienting.

When we neglect prayer, we dis-invite God out of our circumstance and workplace

Seeking God, then, takes a simple commitment to prioritize. We must carve away time from career, business, and the many things that tug at us. We must apply our skills of organization and prioritizing to our prayer life, lest we become spiritually sluggish. I remember reading in the Bible,

[15]The lazy man buries his hand in the bowl; It wearies him to bring it back to his mouth. Prov. 26:15 (NKJV)

I thought, "That's my prayer life!" I could start but couldn't seem to finish. I was inspired to overcome sluggishness by meditating on the examples of several people in the Bible. I call them my heroes of importunity. Importunity is being "troublesomely urgent or persistent in requesting; pressingly entreating." Importunity was one of Jesus' primary teachings on prayer.

The first hero of importunity appears in Jesus' teaching on prayer in the parable of the persistent friend. Jesus said because of the friend's *importunity*, he will get an answer (Luke 11:8).

Another hero is Jacob, who wrestled with God and prevailed because he knew he could get an answer.

We must apply our skills of organization and prioritizing to our prayer life, lest we become spiritually sluggish

The Syrophoenician woman (Matt 15:21-28) is another hero of importunity. She came to Jesus to ask for healing for her daughter. Jesus refused, intending to draw out her faith. She replied, "Even the dogs get the crumbs that fall off the table." Amazing! She was "troublesomely urgent and persistent in requesting, pressingly entreating." Jesus responded, "So great a faith I have not seen in all of Israel."

Blind Bartimaeus (Mark 10:46-52, Luke 18:35-43) is a terrific hero of importunity. When he heard Jesus was coming by, he became the most annoying person in the area, shouting, "Jesus, Son of David, have mercy on me!" The disciples came over to shush him up, but he only became more "troublesomely urgent and persistent in requesting, pressingly entreating." He refused to let his window of opportunity pass.

The widow in Jesus' parable in Luke 18 is a hero of importunity. Even when the unrighteous judge refused her, she continued to entreat him. She was "troublesomely urgent and persistent in requesting, pressingly entreating."

Importunity is one of the single most important understandings of prayer as taught by Jesus. Many times in my life, I have been hit with difficulty, where I needed an answer from God. In these times, my wife and I agreed to pray together three times a day: before I left for work. At lunch when I came home, and before bed. At these times we were never very creative – we usually prayed the same prayers, but we continued to entreat our heavenly Father. Looking back, most of those times God came through for us. We prayed with persistence, because we were convinced we could get an answer.

> **Importunity is one of the single most important understandings of prayer as taught by Jesus**

3 Pillars of Prayer

There are three pillars of understanding that help us to build a vibrant prayer life:

1) God knows and cares – we must never think otherwise. Over and over and over, Jesus made this point when teaching on prayer (Matt 6:25-34, Matt 7:7-11, Luke 11:11-13, Luke 18:1-8). He told us to ask, and continue asking; to seek and continue seeking; to knock and continue knocking, because He cares for us, and He wants to answer us (Matt 7:7-11, Luke 11:11-13).

2) Nobody is worthy enough to ask. None of my heroes of importunity were worthy. None had a "right" to receive. None of them came on legal grounds. They simply asked as children, knowing God would smile on them.

3) Importunity and persistence work. Why did Jesus speak His parables on prayer? The scriptures tell us plainly: "He

men always ought to pray and not lose heart

spoke a parable to them, *that men always ought to pray and not lose heart*." (Luke 18:1) We can get an answer if we don't lose heart and give up.

Taking our Place on the Wall

Marketplace Christians are called to be priests in the workplace, to cry out to God and prevail in matters close to His heart. I often hear Marketplace Christians pray for the fire to return to their hearts. One day as I was praying this very prayer, God brought me to Proverbs 26:20:

The wood for the fire of our hearts is prayer

"for lack of wood the fire goes out." How obvious! How simple! It is amazing God would put such an obvious thought in the Bible. The wood for the fire of our hearts is prayer. Most of us don't need fire — we have plenty of embers — but we do need wood. We need to pray. We need to schedule a regular prayer meeting with God and show up for it. We need to ask with importunity, growing stronger in the knowledge that when we ask, we'll receive. As we grow strong in prayer, we'll become priests in our workplaces.

But we must always keep the dangers of money and the marketplace squarely in view. We'll discuss those dangers next.

CHAPTER NINE:

tending the gardens of our hearts

As confident as we should be in our calling and purpose in the marketplace, we must not be naïve about its dangers. Jesus said,

> *23I tell you the truth, it is hard for a rich man to enter the kingdom of heaven. (Matt 19:23, NIV)*

Many marketplace saints invite disaster by not tending the gardens of their hearts. The marketplace is a spiritual minefield. The scriptures speak in no uncertain terms about the dangers of money. Jesus coined the phrase, "the deceitfulness of riches":

> *19...the deceitfulness of riches, and the desires for other things enter in and choke the word, and it becomes unfruitful. Mark 4:19 (NASB)*

Deceit promises one thing but delivers another. Riches are indeed deceitful. In a museum in Deadwood, South Dakota, is this inscription, left by a prospector: "I lost my gun. I lost my horse. I am out of food. The Indians are after me. But I've got all the gold I can carry." Hardly a person exists who does not believe money will solve his or her problems. But Jesus said it was deceitful.

I recently had a conversation with two very wealthy Christians. They were sharing the pains of bearing the burden of wealth. One said, "People come to me and ask me to pray for them to be wealthy – they have no idea what they are asking for. How do I know what I am supposed to do with this money? I have thousands of people approach me with needs; but who should I give to? What if I don't give to someone that I am supposed to

The scriptures are not optimistic about having wealth and riches

and they suffer? What if I give it away and it just ends up squandered? People close to me look to me as their source and provider instead of God. How do I say 'no' to people I care about? What if I wrongly give to someone and I destroy their lives?" He added remorsefully, "Through unwise giving I destroyed a church." The other man nodded and said, "I destroyed two churches."

I have been poor and I have been rich. There were years when I worked two jobs and couldn't afford anything but to pay our bills. There were years when I was worth tens of millions of dollars. I have seen the blessings and curses of wealth and poverty. Both are burdensome – as the scripture says, "Give me neither poverty nor riches" (Prov. 30:8).

The scriptures are not optimistic about having wealth and riches. When I had nothing, I read those scriptures in disbelief – to me wealth seemed to be the universal answer. When I became wealthy, I saw it in a completely different light.

Let me point out some of the mines I've discovered in the minefield of wealth, and then we'll see how to avoid them.

Wealth Creates False Friends

⁴ *Wealth adds many friends,*
   But a poor man is separated from his friend.
Prov. 19:4 (NASB)

²⁰ *The poor is hated even by his neighbor,*
   But those who love the rich are many.
Prov. 14:20 (NASB)

When I was wealthy and well-known in the city, everybody wanted a piece of me. Everybody "loved" me and pursued me. In meetings, articles and letters, I was continually flattered. But many people I thought were friends lost their interest in me when I no longer had a position of power.

When you are wealthy or powerful, people seek your favor. It's easy to tell what's in some people's hearts, but with others it can be difficult. One wealthy believer was moving to a different city. His pastor, who had become a close friend, became angry and said, "What about how I have ministered to you? You can't just *leave!*" Clearly, his "friendship" had been motivated by something else –

he was expecting to be repaid someday. That's the essence of false friendship.

Wealth is a False Trust

As a wealthy person it is easy to believe we are safe from the ailments of mankind. This confidence tends to produce self-reliance so that we have no need for God:

15 The rich man's wealth is his fortress,
The ruin of the poor is their poverty.
Prov. 10:15 (NASB)

11 A rich man's wealth is his strong city,
And like a high wall in his own imagination.
Prov. 18:11 (NASB)

Wealthy people usually drift away from trust in God because they no longer have to trust Him. It's easier to trust in wealth, to be spiritually lethargic and self-reliant, than to cultivate dependence on God.

Wealth is a False Hope for Deliverance

Wealth promises to deliver us from difficulties, but in fact will not:

4 Riches do not profit in the day of wrath,
But righteousness delivers from death.
Prov. 11:4 (NASB)

^{28} *He who trusts in his riches will fall,*
  But the righteous will flourish like the green leaf.
Prov. 11:28 (NASB)

Wealth Brings Increased Cares

^{8}*Being kidnapped and held for ransom never worries the poor man! Prov. 13:8 (TLB)*

As a dirt-poor college student, I had little more than a bicycle, a beanbag chair and a Bible to my name. As I have grown older, life has become vastly more demanding. The more money you have, the more it becomes a full-time job taking care of your possessions and protecting your investments.

Wealth Spawns Pride

^{23} *The poor man utters supplications,*
    But the rich man answers roughly.
Prov. 18:23 (NASB)

^{11} *The rich man is wise in his own eyes,*
    But the poor who has understanding sees through him.
Prov. 28:11 (NASB)

As I became wealthier and more important, I became increasingly prideful. I rubbed shoulders with many extremely successful people. In many cases they were arrogant, demeaning and mean-spirited. Success often breeds an ugly arrogance.

Wealth Brings Increased Responsibility and Accountability

⁷ *The rich rules over the poor,*
And the borrower becomes the lender's slave.
Prov. 22:7 (NASB)

The rich will find themselves in places of authority; but authority is a double-edged sword which brings increased responsibility and accountability.

Wealth is Fickle

⁴ *Do not weary yourself to gain wealth,*
Cease from your consideration of it.
⁵ *When you set your eyes on it, it is gone.*
For wealth certainly makes itself wings
Like an eagle that flies toward the heavens.
Prov. 23:4-5 (NASB)

While wealth seems tangible and reliable, it can never be relied up. Businesses fail, and drop in value; stocks and investments fail; and sometimes even currencies fail, like in Germany in the 1920s.

Wealth is a False Storehouse

⁶ *Man is a mere phantom as he goes to and fro:*
He bustles about, but only in vain;
he heaps up wealth, not knowing who will get it.

Psa. 39:6 (NIV)

In the blink of an eye this life is over and everything we accumulated in this life – wealth, prestige, positions of honor, etc. – are completely vaporized. There is no place we can put wealth so that it cannot be destroyed – except giving it to God and building for the next life.

Four Forms of Greed

Jesus expounded on the perils of wealth in the parable of the rich man in Luke 12:13-21.

[13]Someone in the crowd said to Him, "Teacher, tell my brother to divide the family inheritance with me." [14]But He said to him, "Man, who appointed Me a judge or arbitrator over you?" [15]Then He said to them, "Beware, and <u>be on your guard against every form of greed</u>; for not even when one has an abundance does his life consist of his possessions." [16]And He told them a parable, saying, "The land of a rich man was very productive. [17]"And he began reasoning to himself, saying, 'What shall I do, since I have no place to store my crops?' [18]"Then he said, 'This is what I will do: I will tear down my barns and build larger ones, and there I will store all my grain and my goods. [19]'And I will say to my soul, "Soul, you have many goods laid up for many years to come; take your ease, eat, drink and be merry."' [20]"But God said to him, 'You fool! This very night your soul is required of you; and now who will own what you have prepared?' [21]"So is the man who stores up treasure for himself, and is not rich toward God." Luke 12:13-21 (NASB)

He said we should "be aware" and "be on guard" against every form of greed. This literally means to "post a guard" in our hearts and vigilantly check our motives and desires. Greed is subtle and takes many forms. Let's consider the four forms of greed that were mentioned by Jesus:

Desires for Other Things

We all desire a long list of things: the love of others, a career, success, recognition, significance, promotion, a bigger house, a newer car and so on. These things are not evil in themselves, but they become evil if they take precedence in our heart. Because we live in the world, it is inevitable that we will think about earthly matters. But we must guard against "values creep," when our values slowly morph into worldly values. Like David, we must be men and women of "one thing" (Ps. 27:4). Everything in our hearts must be secondary to Jesus.

He is jealous over our affections and will destroy any other loves that have captured our heart

God is a jealous God; He will not stand for our hearts to be given to other things. He is jealous over our affections and will destroy any other loves that have captured our heart. If we set up another love, another primary reward in our hearts, we can be assured that Jesus will come as a jealous lover to destroy it.

Jesus Himself is our primary reward – not His gifts, His ministry, His blessing, but Him personally. Knowing Him is the greatest gift

He could give us. It is for this He joyfully suffered and died. Before Jesus died, he prayed for us:

26I have made you known to them, and will continue to make you known in order that the love you have for me may be in them and that I myself may be in them." (John 17:26 – NIV)

The Father's primary goal in heaven and earth is to glorify the Son – and to form a people that love Jesus as the Father loves Him. The Father will not rest until this love is manifest in His bride. Jesus will not wed a slave, but a bride that is in love with Him.

> **Jesus Himself is our primary reward – not His gifts, His ministry, His blessing, but Him personally**

What is the inheritance of the saints? Power? Success? Ruling and reigning in the new earth? Paradise? Our primary inheritance is Jesus Christ, the Person – our Bridegroom:

20Then the LORD said to Aaron, "You shall have no inheritance in their land nor own any portion among them; I am your portion and your inheritance among the sons of Israel. (Num. 18:20 – NASB)

If we desire a different primary inheritance, we have terribly misunderstood the gospel; and we are setting ourselves up for a grave disappointment. The scriptures speak of this in 1 Timothy in the context of the pursuit of money; but it could just as easily be recognition, promotion or career:

9But those who want [something besides Jesus] fall into temptation and a snare and many foolish and harmful desires which plunge men into ruin and destruction. ^{10}*… some by longing for [other things] have wandered away from the faith and pierced themselves with many griefs. 1 Tim. 6:9-10 (Paraphrased from NASB)*

To pursue anything but Jesus as your inheritance is to destine yourself for disappointment and hurt. I have met scores of people who are angry at the Lord. They believe they deserve something different from what they have received. Without exception, they have another primary reward besides Jesus. I have never heard one of these embittered souls say, "I so wanted Jesus, but He was withheld from me." They do not realize that their disappointment and hurt is a direct result of their ungodly attachment to another love. As a jealous lover, Jesus came and destroyed the object of their affection because it supplanted their love for Him. We gave Him permission to do this when we gave Him our vows of love. If Jesus is our primary reward, then losses of secondary things only draw us closer to him.

> **To pursue anything but Jesus as your inheritance is to destine yourself for disappointment and hurt**

We cannot set our heart on any earthly inheritance at all. While God may give us an earthly blessing, it is not guaranteed. The essence of our great gospel is forgoing earthly reward to gain a heavenly reward. *Hurt and disappointment is proof that we wanted something from God besides Himself.* Jesus inherited nothing on earth. On earth, as believers, this is our only true gain: that we get to know Him, walk with Him and love Him.

Self-Indulgence

Another sign of greed is self-indulgence. The rich man in the parable said to himself, "take your ease, eat, drink and be merry" (Luke 12:19). As God blesses us, it is natural to use some gain for our own desires. This is neither evil nor unscriptural. The scripture says, "You should not muzzle the ox while he is threshing" (Deut. 25:4, 1 Cor. 9:9, 1 Tim. 5:18).

However, as we spend for our own pleasure, we can become gradually addicted to self-gratification. Indulgence is defined as "an inability to resist the gratification of whims and desires; a disposition to yield to wishes." We must strengthen our ability to restrain ourselves.

We cannot seek a life of ease. If this is our aim, we are making a grave error. The rich man in the parable sought a life of ease. Another rich man, appearing in a parable in Luke 16, also sought a life of ease.

> **We cannot seek a life of ease. If this is our aim, we are making a grave error**

[16]*There was a rich man who was dressed in purple and fine linen and lived in luxury every day. Luke 16:19 (NIV)*

In my younger days I dreamed of a life of ease. But to seek a life of ease is to seek earthly reward instead of heavenly. It means we have ceased from our spiritual calling. It makes sense that in Jesus' parable of Luke 12, God took the rich man's life – it no longer had any spiritual purpose.

Self-indulgence and the pursuit of pleasure create spiritual lethargy:

¹⁴"The seed which fell among the thorns, these are the ones who have heard, and as they go on their way they are choked with worries and <u>riches and pleasures of this life</u>, and bring no fruit to maturity. Luke 8:14 (NASB)

In the parables of Luke 12 and 16, the rich men became spiritually lethargic. When we become self-indulgent we let our wealth create in us self-sufficiency: like the Laodiceans we say, "I am rich, and have become wealthy, and have need of nothing" (Rev. 3:17, NASB). This is a dangerous spiritual state, because a self-sufficient person is one who has no need of God – they are sufficient in themselves.

Self-indulgence and the pursuit of pleasure create spiritual lethargy

God gave an eye-opening insight into what actually happened at Sodom and Gomorrah when He spoke through the prophet Ezekiel,

⁴⁹Behold, this was the guilt of your sister Sodom: she and her daughters had arrogance, <u>abundant food and careless ease</u>, but she did not help the poor and needy. ⁵⁰Thus they were haughty and committed abominations before Me. (Ezek. 16:49-50, NASB)

Surprisingly, God did not charge their overt sin, but a deeper root cause: "arrogance, abundant food and careless ease." Self-indulgence, self-sufficiency and seeking a life of ease bring some of the most dire warnings in scripture: Sodom and Gomorrah were destroyed by fire; the Laodiceans were about to be vomited out of God's mouth; the rich man in Luke 12 lost his life; and the rich man in Luke 16 ended up in the torment of hell. *These dangers provide a quick method of dooming your soul.*

If that doesn't put you on guard, nothing will!

Insensitivity to the Needs of Others

Sodom and Gomorrah's sin is also further expounded: "she did not help the poor and needy." The rich man in Luke 16 ignored Lazarus, a poor beggar who lived outside his gate. In the Sermon on the Mount, we are told to "give to him who asks" of us (Matt. 5:42). John the Baptist told us, "The man with two tunics should share with him who has none, and the one who has food should do the same" (Luke 3:11). In defining the second greatest commandment, "loving our neighbor," Jesus told us to be sensitive to the needy in our path.

> **Surprisingly, God did not charge their overt sin, but a deeper root cause: "arrogance, abundant food and careless ease."**

The Bible speaks with a single voice when it says our hearts should be always tender to the needs of others. It's easy to find reasons not to give: "I don't know where to give;" "It will just be squandered;" "I'll hold it for now and give it later;" or "It won't have any impact." All these reasons can be legitimate in the short-term; but we must solve these problems and find a way to be givers. If we continually find ways to overlook the needs of others, we have succumbed to greed.

Riches Without a Cause

It is a danger signal if we have increased wealth without an increased cause. This happened to the rich man in Luke 12. He found himself increasingly blessed, but his response was, *"What shall I do?"* He had no cause, no greater purpose for his wealth. We can tell when we have no cause because we will do what the rich man did: we will save more and more. *If we have no cause motivated by a heart of love, then our cause will always become self.* We rejoice in blessing and growth but not for what it will do for others.

> It is a danger signal if we have increased wealth without an increased cause

We must ask ourselves, *What is the purpose of our wealth?* One day we will stand before God and answer for our stewardship. As our wealth increases, so should our passion for a cause – whatever it is.

Developing a Clean Heart

How can we keep our hearts from being captured by the deceitfulness of riches? Thankfully, Jesus said regarding the rich entering the Kingdom of Heaven, "With God all things are possible" (Matt. 19:23-26). Here are the steps to developing a clean heart towards wealth.

Admit Greed

Start by being honest. *There is not a one among us who is not tainted to some degree by greed.* Don't pretend your heart is unaffected. Neutralize iniquity by bringing it into the light.

Engage Our Hearts in Pursuit of God

It is impossible to maintain a heart of purity without persistently pursuing God. I tend to succumb to the impurities in my heart when I am pursuing God the least. Ironically, at those same times I am least aware of my iniquity, making it doubly dangerous. If we are not pursuing intimacy with God, we are drifting away from Him, succumbing to "spiritual entropy," and growing vulnerable to the entrapments of the enemy.

> **It is impossible to maintain a heart of purity without persistently pursuing God**

Embrace the "Fasted Lifestyle"

One powerful method of spiritual warfare against the distractions and dissipation of life is what Mike Bickle calls the "fasted lifestyle." This means forgoing some of todays wants in order to lay hold of God. The fasted lifestyle can mean giving up anything: meals, television, a new house, a new car, time or money. This lifestyle is "spiritual violence" (Matt. 11:12) against self-absorption. It breaks the pleasure-oriented lifestyle that's considered normal by Western standards. It informs our soul that there is a God, and that we are serving Him.

Gary Ginter, the "treasure bringer" mentioned in Chapter 2 has embraced the fasted lifestyle. Though he has made hundreds of millions of dollars in his business, he lives with his family in a small three-bedroom house in a poor neighborhood. He drives an old car and lives a completely austere life so he can give more to the purposes of God. He calls his lifestyle, "warfare lifestyle."

Cultivate Generosity

Generosity is the greatest weapon against greed, and the antidote that most often appears in scripture. Jesus said,

[19] *"Do not lay up for yourselves treasures on earth, where moth and rust destroy and where thieves break in and steal;* [20]*but lay up for yourselves treasures in heaven, where neither moth nor rust destroys and where thieves do not break in and steal.* [21]*For where your treasure is, there your heart will be also. Matt. 6:19-21 (NKJV)*

> **By simply taking some of our earthly treasure and converting it to heavenly treasure by giving it away, we can control our hearts**

If our heart follows our treasure, then our lifestyle should be one of giving versus accumulation. According to this verse, we can keep our hearts firmly anchored in God simply by giving. This scripture makes it amazingly simple to lay up heavenly treasure and keep our hearts pure. *By simply taking some of our earthly treasure and converting it to heavenly treasure by giving it away, we can control our hearts and reap eternal rewards.* It astounds me that we can cash in temporary wealth for eternal wealth. We'd be fools not to. You can't own earthly wealth forever anyway. Anything you own will one day be given to someone else — that's the nature of temporal wealth. *But we have a grand opportunity while on this earth to trade the temporal for the eternal by simply giving it away.* Imagine that the U.S. government announced that at the end of the month green dollars would be worthless, and new red dollars would be our currency. We would be fools to keep green dollars. In the same way, God gives us the opportunity to trade the worthless for the eternal. But if we wait too long, it will all be given away for us, and we'll have nothing in heaven to show for it.

Jesus gave a parable that expounds this principle even further – the parable of the unrighteous steward:

[1]Now He was also saying to the disciples, "There was a rich man who had a manager, and this manager was reported to him as squandering his possessions. [2]"And he called him and said to him, 'What is this I hear about you? Give an accounting of your management, for you can no longer be manager.' [3]"The manager said to himself, 'What shall I do, since my master is taking the management away from me? I am not strong enough to dig; I am ashamed to beg. [4]'I know what I shall do, so that when I am removed from the management people will welcome me into their homes.' [5]"And he summoned each one of his master's debtors, and he began saying to the first, 'How much do you owe my master?' [6]"And he said, 'A hundred measures of oil.' And he said to him, 'Take your bill, and sit down quickly and write fifty.' [7]"Then he said to another, 'And how much do you owe?' And he said, 'A hundred measures of wheat.' He said* to him, 'Take your bill, and write eighty.' [8]"And his master praised the unrighteous manager

because he had acted shrewdly; for the sons of this age are more shrewd in relation to their own kind than the sons of light. [9]"And I say to you, make friends for yourselves by means of the wealth of unrighteousness, so that when it fails, they will receive you into the eternal dwellings. Luke 16:1-9 (NASB)

The rich man is God, the one who really owns our resources. The manager is us. The manager's stewardship was coming to an end, meaning that all earthly wealth is temporal. The steward began to realize he was ill-prepared for the next phase of his life, just as we might find ourselves ill-prepared for the afterlife. He began to trade this temporal wealth — wealth that didn't even belong to him — for heavenly wealth. Instead of being angry, the master praised him. Paul summed up the best approach in 1Timothy:

> **The rich man is God, the one who really owns our resources. The manager is us.**

[17]Instruct those who are rich in this present world not to be conceited or to fix their hope on the uncertainty of riches, but on God, who richly supplies us with all things to enjoy. [18]Instruct them to do good, to be rich in good works, to be generous and ready to share, [19]storing up for themselves the treasure of a good foundation for the future, so that they may take hold of that which is life indeed. 1 Tim. 6:17-19 (NASB)

Find Our "Love Cause"

A lot of Christians try to do good and sacrifice of themselves, but generosity and "doing good" can never be sustained without true love. Going through the motions and putting external controls or boundaries on ourselves can't sustain our generosity. We need a heart of true love for the cause we are giving to.

What loving mother could sell her child into slavery for a million dollars? Or a billion? Or a trillion? My wife would beat with a stick anyone who even attempted the offer. As the Song of Solomon says, "If a man were to give all the riches of his house for love, it would be utterly despised" (Song 8:7). Jonathan could not betray David, his friend, even for the entire Kingdom, because he loved him. *Love is the single most powerful force in the human heart – where true love is, no other power can even begin to contend.*

All of our efforts at self-sacrificing and generosity are unsustainable without a heart of love. Love easily overpowers every other force — the spirit of mammon, selfishness, greed and ambition, to name a few. *Mature love makes the heart incorruptible.* You might try to stand against the spirit of mammon in your own strength, and you'll never win. But with true love in your heart, you'll win every time.

> **All of our efforts at self-sacrificing and generosity are unsustainable without a heart of love**

Our first "love cause" must be the cross, and our beloved Savior. Our second love cause must be the needs of others.

[27]He who gives to the poor will lack nothing, but he who closes his eyes to them receives many curses. Prov. 28:27 (NIV)

A few years ago I went on a missions trip to Cuba. The Cuban saints are in great persecution and hardship, often imprisoned, stolen from, harassed and living in dire poverty. But their faith is strong and their passion burns hot. They work tirelessly without complaint. Whenever my heart drifts back to its natural Scrooge-like state when it comes to giving, I only have to remember the Cubans, and I simply *must give*. They have become a love cause of mine.

Often the needs of others are so incessant, bottomless and intractable it is natural for us to insulate ourselves from them

Often the needs of others are so incessant, bottomless and intractable, it is natural for us to insulate ourselves from them, simply to spare ourselves the hopelessness. But we must do exactly the opposite: we must continually expose ourselves to the needs of others and ask God to tenderize our hearts by showing us His heart for the people and their situations. Instead of running and hiding from the needs of others, we must put ourselves in the way of their need.

If you have no love cause, ask God to give you one ... or two, or three. Then you can fulfill the second greatest commandment, loving your neighbor as yourself.

In all of these ways, we can tend to the gardens of our hearts, walking confidently and wisely in the marketplace, avoiding the minefields that come with wealth.

CHAPTER TEN

the charge of joseph

For many years I puzzled over a bizarre reference to Joseph in Hebrews 11, the "hall of faith" chapter:

> *[22]By faith Joseph, when his end was near, spoke about the exodus of the Israelites from Egypt and gave instructions about his bones. Heb. 11:22 (NIV)*

Why would Joseph care about where his bones were taken after he died? As I was meditating on this one day, the meaning hit me. This was Joseph's way of declaring the true location of his heart. As a forerunner of Marketplace Christians, Joseph lived fully in the "marketplace" of Egypt, a wealthy and comfortable land. Joseph's people were multiplying and prospering, partaking of the "good life" of riches, cuisine, art, craftsmanship, learning, science, government, culture and extravagance of Egypt – the most advanced and fabulous culture on the planet at the time. It is clear why God sent them there: to become strong and to learn to build a great nation under the tutelage of the greatest nation yet known.

But there was a problem: along with the greatness, there was sensuality and indulgence. The fabulous riches were seductive and could cause them to forget who they were, and to forget the promises of God, which seemed far off. Complacency and assimilation threatened the purpose for which they were designed.

But Egypt was not God's final destination for the people of Israel. It was merely the place where they would grow strong — from seventy-five nomadic ranchers to a great nation by the time Moses led them out. By giving instructions about his bones, Joseph was proclaiming that even though he poured his life into the success of Egypt — which for us represents the marketplace — his real purpose was to fulfill the promises of God. I can imagine him saying before he died, "It is God's plan that we become a great nation in the Promised Land, as was told to our forefathers. Until then we must make the most of this opportunity in Egypt. Though Egypt is our home today, it is not our destiny. We are in Egypt, but we must not become Egyptians.

By his astonishing declaration about his bones, Joseph proclaimed he lived for the promises of God rather than temporal earthly gain

"Soon I will die; and though I was great and wealthy in the house of the Pharaoh, and though I have many friends here, this is not my true home. When I die, place my bones in a box and take them with you when you leave this land. Bury them in the land God has promised. Though I will not live to personally see the day of promise, I will still participate in it."

By his astonishing declaration about his bones, Joseph proclaimed he lived for the promises of God rather than temporal earthly gain. He refused to be identified with his accomplishments or the blessings on his life, but only with the promises of God. He proclaimed Egypt was not his true home (nor by implication, theirs), but the Promised Land was – he and they were but strangers and sojourners in the land of Egypt. His bones became a "monument of temporality" to his descendants, reminding them this life was but a warm-up for the life to come, and reminding them that their promised inheritance was in that other life.

Our Real Destiny

Like Joseph, Marketplace Christians are anointed to govern, but we govern in a foreign nation — the marketplace. While we serve with everything we have, our eyes are on another country; we live in awareness of the promises. The exodus that Moses led is a type of the second coming of Christ, when Jesus will confront the powers of darkness and lead His people in great power and wonders. Like Joseph, we want to be a part of that great drama, even if only with our bones.

> We live in the wealthiest, most seductive culture ever to exist on planet earth

We live in the wealthiest, most seductive culture ever to exist on planet earth. We face the same dangers that faced the Israelites in Egypt: we are in *danger of being assimilated* by the world. Every day the pleasures, dissipations, distractions, desires and pursuits of other things war against our soul, seeking to undermine the promises, making them distant, seeking to make us forget who we are and what our true purpose is.

Though we work wholeheartedly in the marketplace, we are commanded to live as strangers on earth, as those just passing through

Where do you want your bones to be buried? Where do you want to leave your legacy? Will your legacy be trophies, bank accounts, homes, boats and automobiles — the passing pleasures the marketplace provides? Or will it be in heaven, where the throng of saints will greet you at the gate, your Father praising and affirming you because you spent your life for love?

Though we work wholeheartedly in the marketplace, we are commanded to live as strangers on earth, as those just passing through:

[17]Since you call on a Father who judges each man's work impartially, <u>live your lives as strangers here</u> in reverent fear. 1 Pet. 1:17 (NIV)

[13]All these people were still living by faith when they died. They did not receive the things promised; they only saw them and welcomed them from a distance. And <u>they admitted that they were aliens and strangers on earth</u>. Heb. 11:13 (NIV)

[11]Dear friends, I urge you, as <u>aliens and strangers</u> in the world, to abstain from sinful desires, which war against your soul. 1 Pet. 2:11 (NIV)

We live and work on this earth, but we have a different inheritance, a different home. Like ambassadors in a foreign land, we do not seek our reward in the land of our service, but in our homeland, and from our King. To seek our reward in the land of our service would be a betrayal of our King, because it is Him we are to be serving and representing. We know our service is short, and we must faithfully discharge the trust He has placed in us, representing Him and His wishes as much as we are able, not our own, until we return home to Him.

> **To seek our reward in the land of our service would be a betrayal of our King**

As Mike Bickle says, "this life is a brief internship for the next." Seventy years is as the blink of an eye in the face of eternity. How we handle this brief internship determines our station and reward in the next. What a shame if we spend our internship for ourselves, offering him nothing in return for his sacrifice, and inheriting eternal life but without reward (1 Cor. 3:13-15). This is the age of faith – it is the only time we will have that can offer him faith – trust without seeing. Once we see him with our eyes, it is no longer by faith.

True Faith

We must have great faith, as Joseph had. Faith is giving up today's temporary reward for tomorrow's eternal reward. It's investing in an unseen world and disinvesting in the seen world. It's placing trust in the invisible realm above the visible realm. It's giving up what is tangible to lay hold of that which is only promised. Such faith honors the One who promises. When we accept Jesus Christ as savior it is dis-investing in human efforts at salvation and investing in His unseen efforts. When we give in faith, it is forgoing earthly reward which we can see, taste

To become spiritual men and women, we must readily trade earthly gain, reward and recognition for heavenly

and feel, in order to attain heavenly reward, which we have never seen, tasted or felt. When we work as for the Lord, it is rejecting the serving of man, by which we would have earthly gain, in order to serve the unseen God, to attain an unseen reward. When martyrs gladly give their lives, it is a willingness to dis-invest in earthly gain in order to attain unseen, unknown heavenly gain. When we pray, we disinvest for a time in human efforts, in order to ask of an invisible God. These activities are all born of faith. All honor God, because we are placing our trust in Him.

To become spiritual men and women, we must readily trade earthly gain, reward and recognition for heavenly. We must embrace earthly loss for heavenly gain. We must eagerly follow Him from a heart of love.

John Wesley was a classical scholar. He loved books and learning, art, music and architecture. Visiting the beautiful grounds of an English nobleman one time Wesley said, "I too have a relish for these things; *but there is another world.*" Let that truth pervade our lives as we passionately pursue our calling and purpose in the marketplace.

order form

Books	Qty	Price	Total
Marketplace Christianity	____	$11.99	_____

Subtotal: _____

Shipping. Add 10% (Minimum $2.00): _____

Tax. (Kansas residents add 7.525%): _____

Total Enclosed (US funds only): _____

Your Name: _____

Address: _____

City, State, Zip: _____

E-Mail Address: _____

Send payment with order to:

New Grid Books
11184 Antioch #354
Overland Park, KS, 66210

Order online at: www.newgridbooks.com. For volume discounts, visit the web site.

about the author

Robert Fraser is the founder and director of the Joseph Company (www.josephcompany.org), a ministry dedicated to restoring a vision for the marketplace.

Prior to the Joseph Company, Robert founded NetSales, Inc., a back-office e-commerce provider for thousands of business customers, including Xerox, Chase Manhattan Bank, and Samsung. Robert raised $44 million in investment capital, and guided the company to an average of 20% month-to-month revenue growth over 6 years, becoming the Kansas City metro area's fastest growing company between 1997 and 1999. In 2000, Robert was awarded the Midwest Region Ernst & Young Entrepreneur of the Year Award.

Robert has also been a technology industry spokesperson, having written dozens of published articles and white papers, and has been a featured speaker at technology gatherings such as Comdex, Networld+Interop, Internet World, Software Publisher's Association, and ABC World News Tonight.

about the
joseph company

The Joseph Company is a ministry of the International House of Prayer in Kansas City (IHOP-KC). Our vision is to release a prophetic understanding of the purposes of God, especially as it relates to the marketplace; release mercy deeds to the nations; impact world leaders with the gospel; and to redeem the marketplace as a place of the activity of the Kingdom of God.

The Joseph Company sponsors conferences and leadership retreats; we sponsor regional chapters and events, and a business prayer network.

If you would like to be released into your marketplace destiny, and receive a deep impartation of the truths spoken of in this book, you should consider attending a Joseph Company Leadership Retreat. Many marketplace leaders have had their lives deeply impacted.

For more information visit www.josephcompany.org.

the international house of prayer

On September 19, 1999, a prayer and worship meeting began in South Kansas City that continues this very hour. For over four years, night-and-day worship with intercession has gone up before the throne of God. Convinced that Jesus is worthy of incessant adoration, men and women of all ages from across the globe are giving themselves to extravagant love expressed through 24/7 prayer. Structured in eighty-four two-hour meetings a week, full teams of musicians, singers, and intercessors lift their voices in praise and supplication, asking God to fulfill His promise and give the nations of the earth to Jesus as His inheritance.

For more information visit www.ihop.org.